GERHARD RICHTER **NOVEMBER**

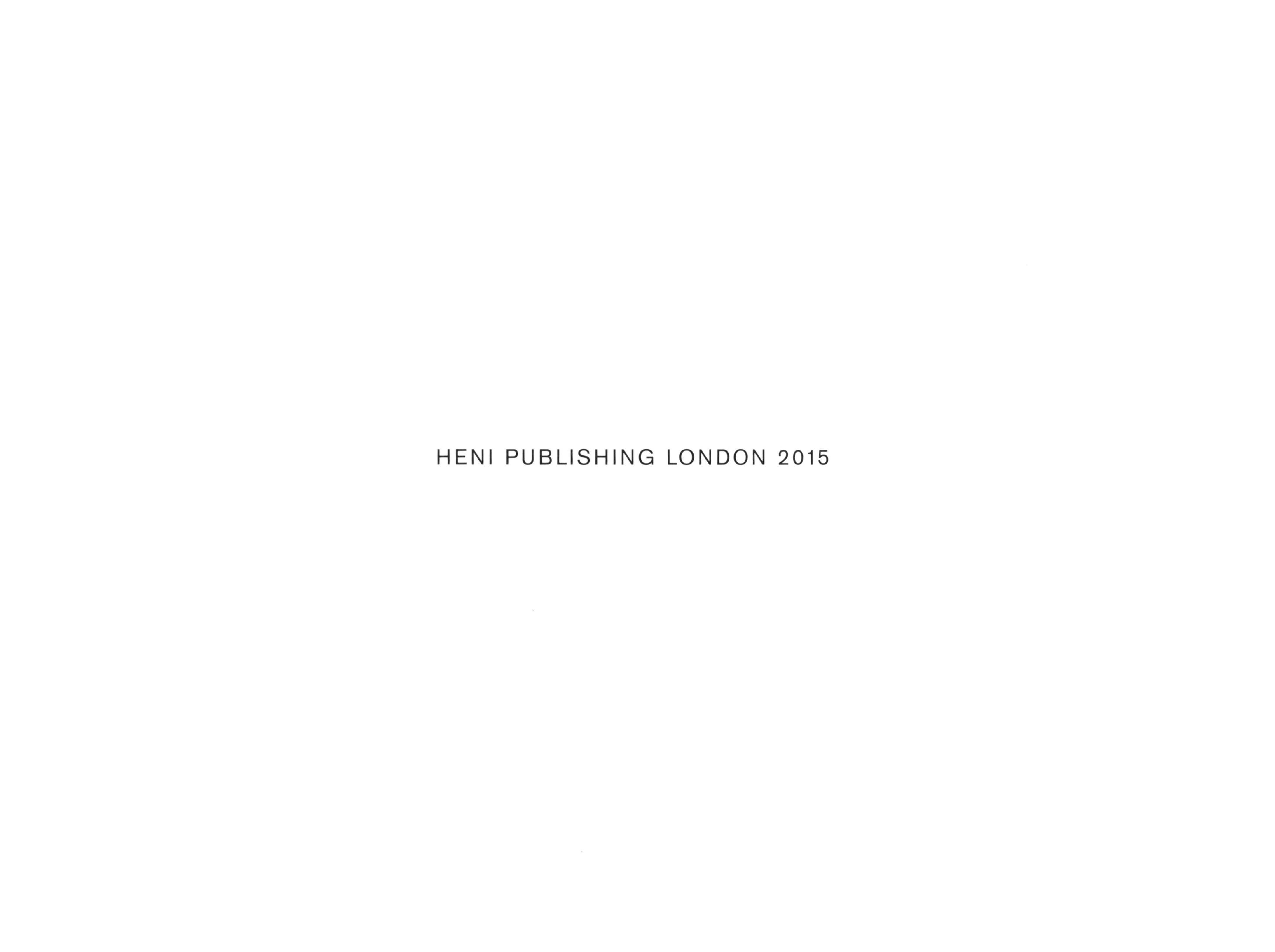

HENI PUBLISHING LONDON 2015

GERHARD RICHTER

NOVEMBER

54 ink drawings
on both sides of 27 sheets,
each 210 × 297 mm
by Gerhard Richter in November 2008

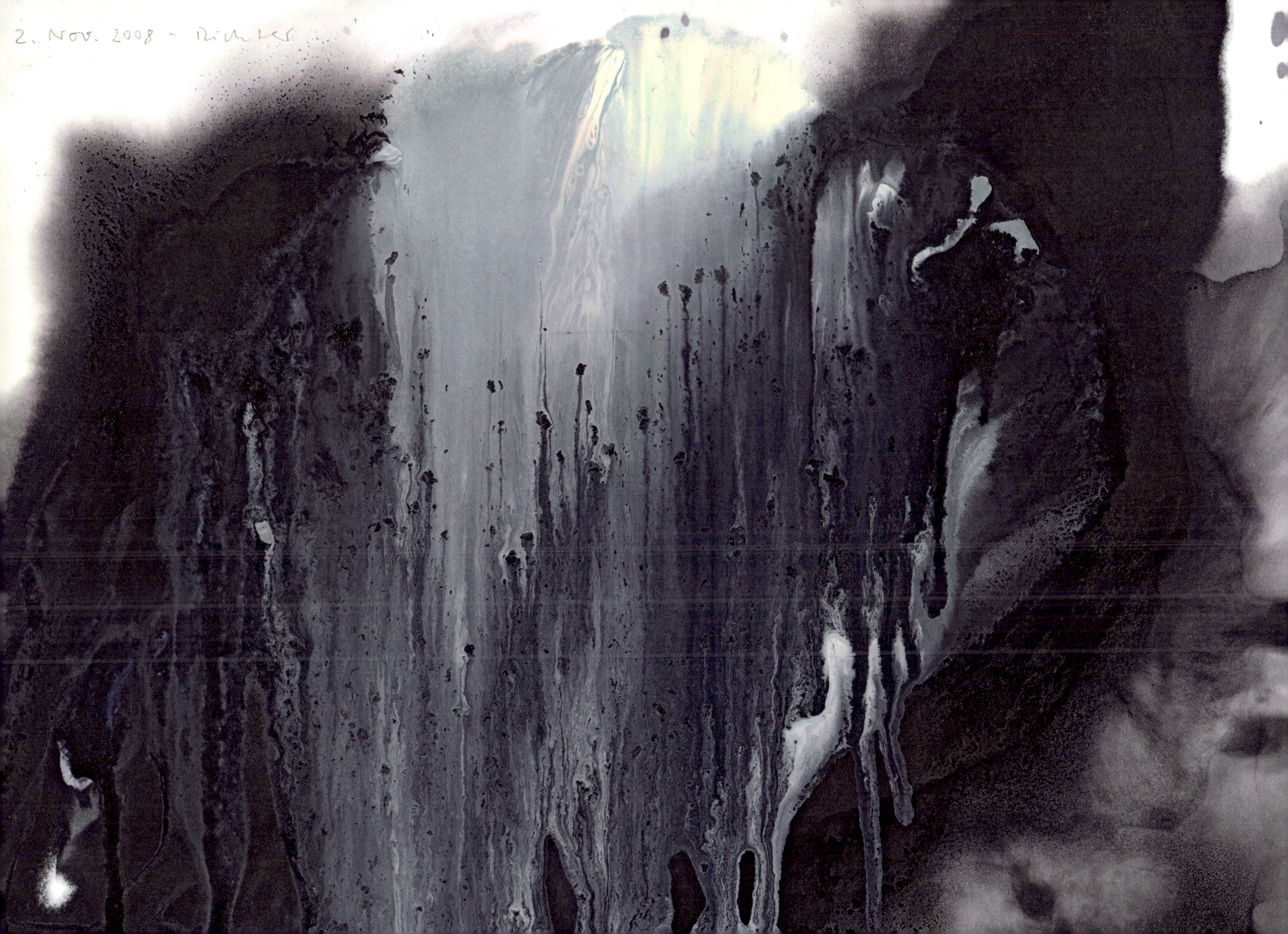
2. Nov. 2008 - Richter

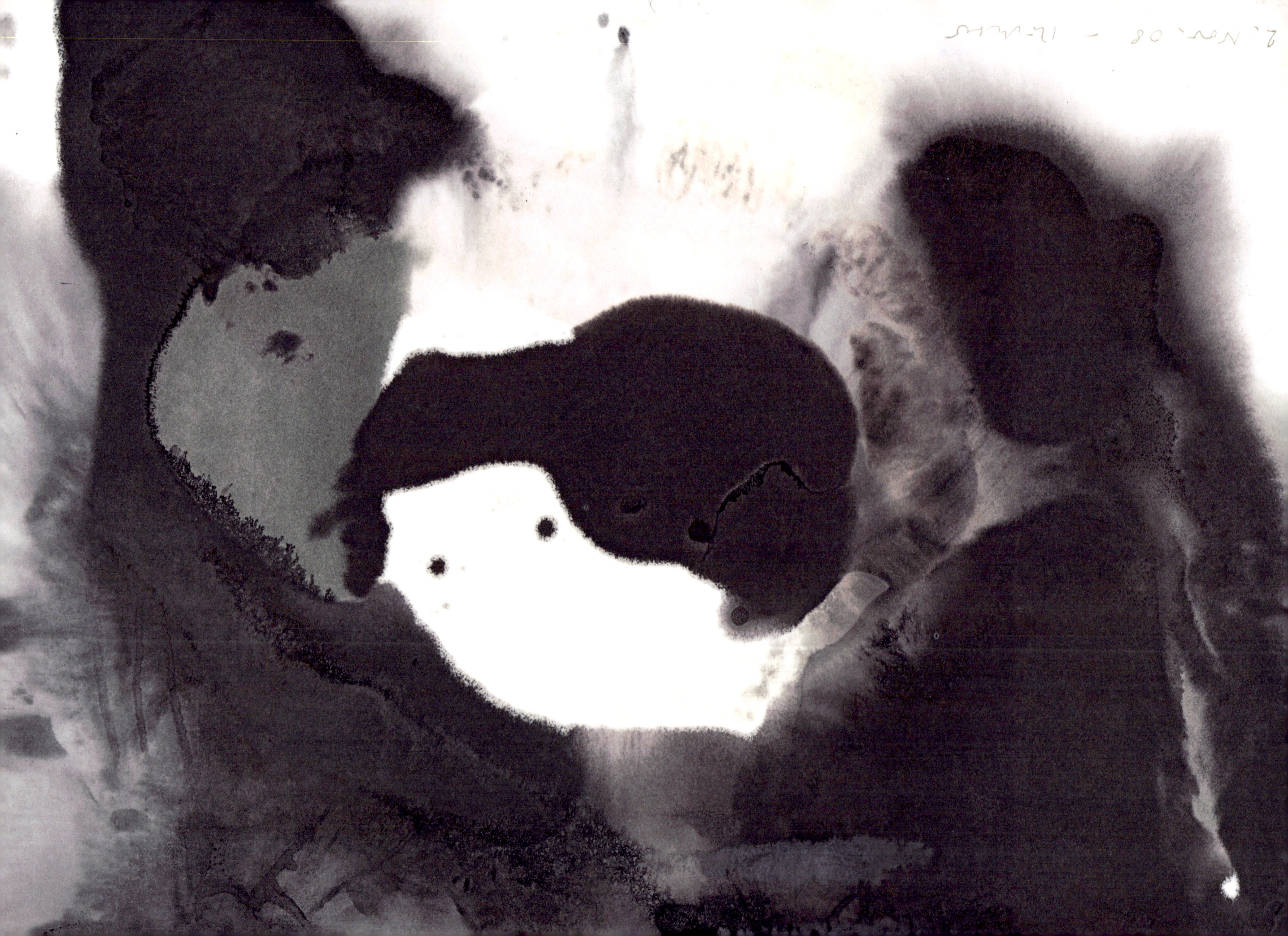

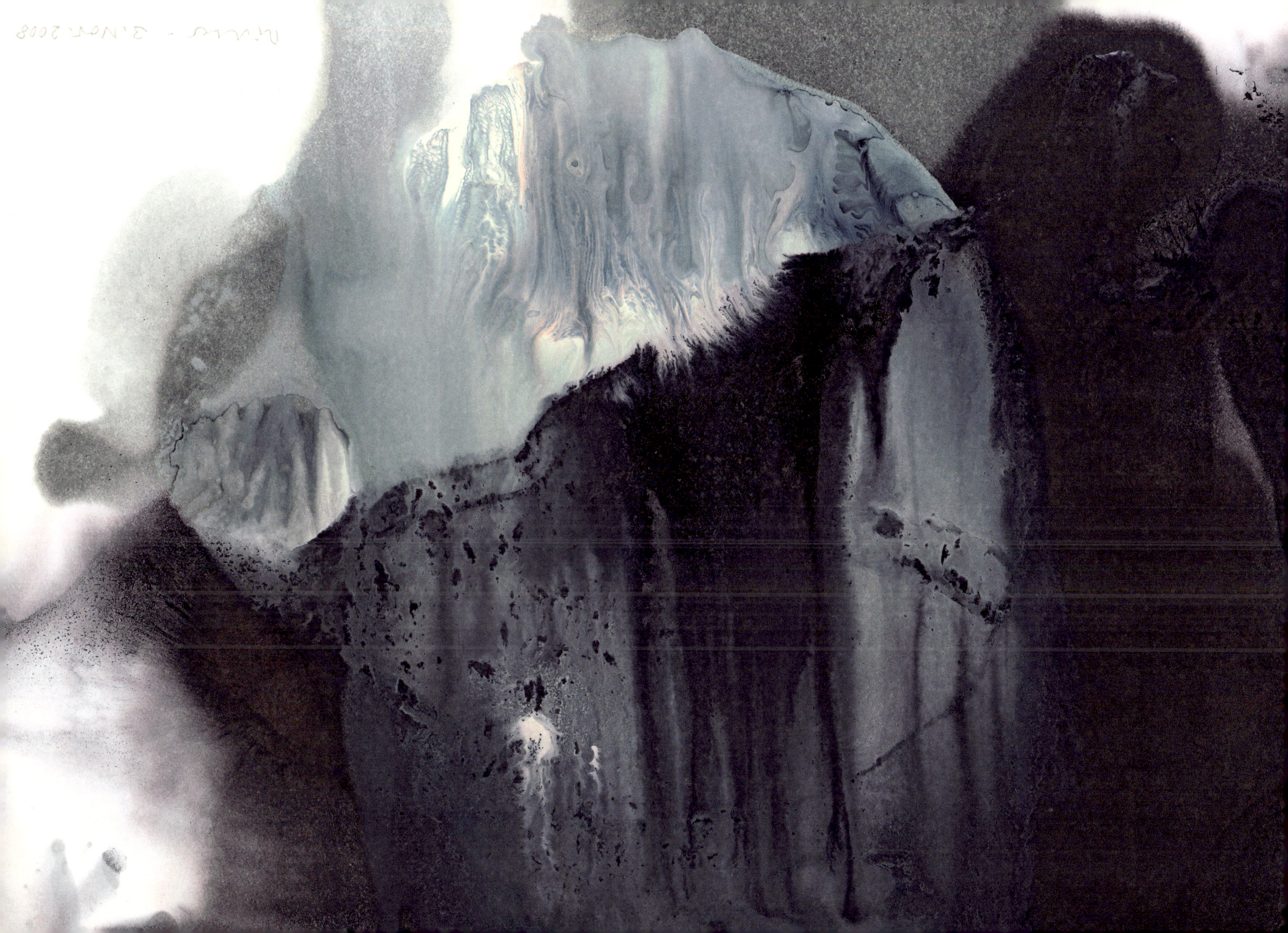

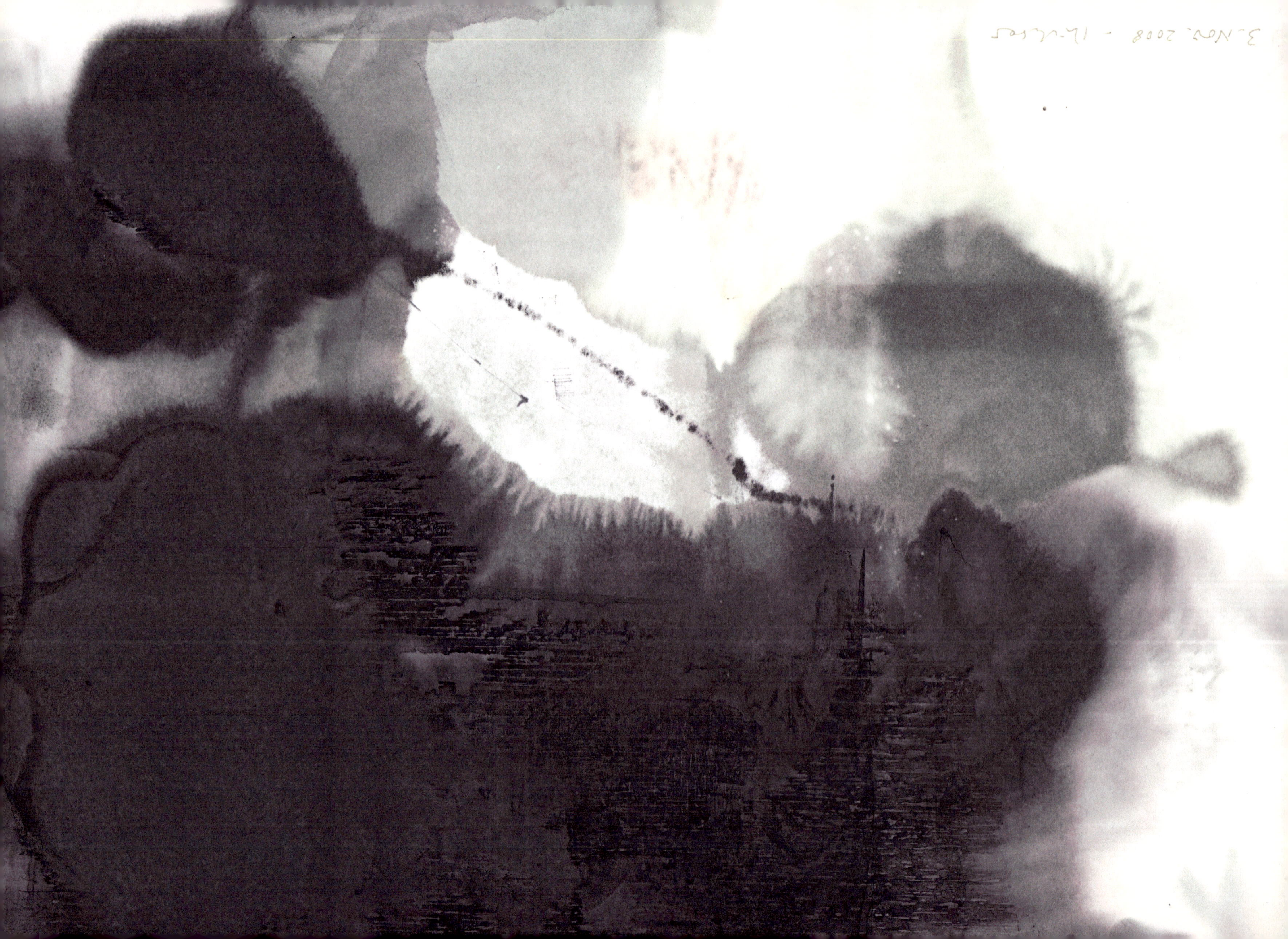

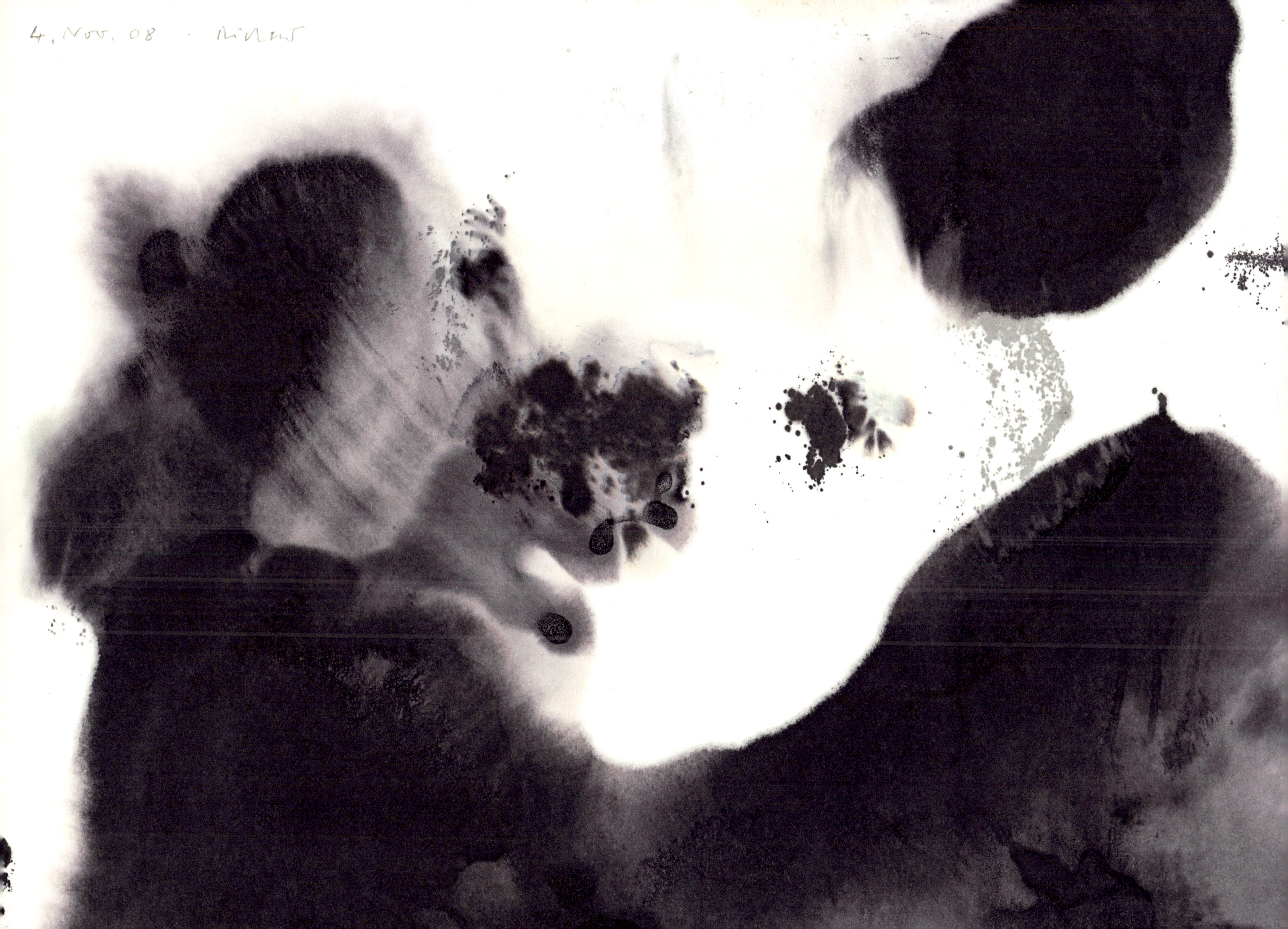

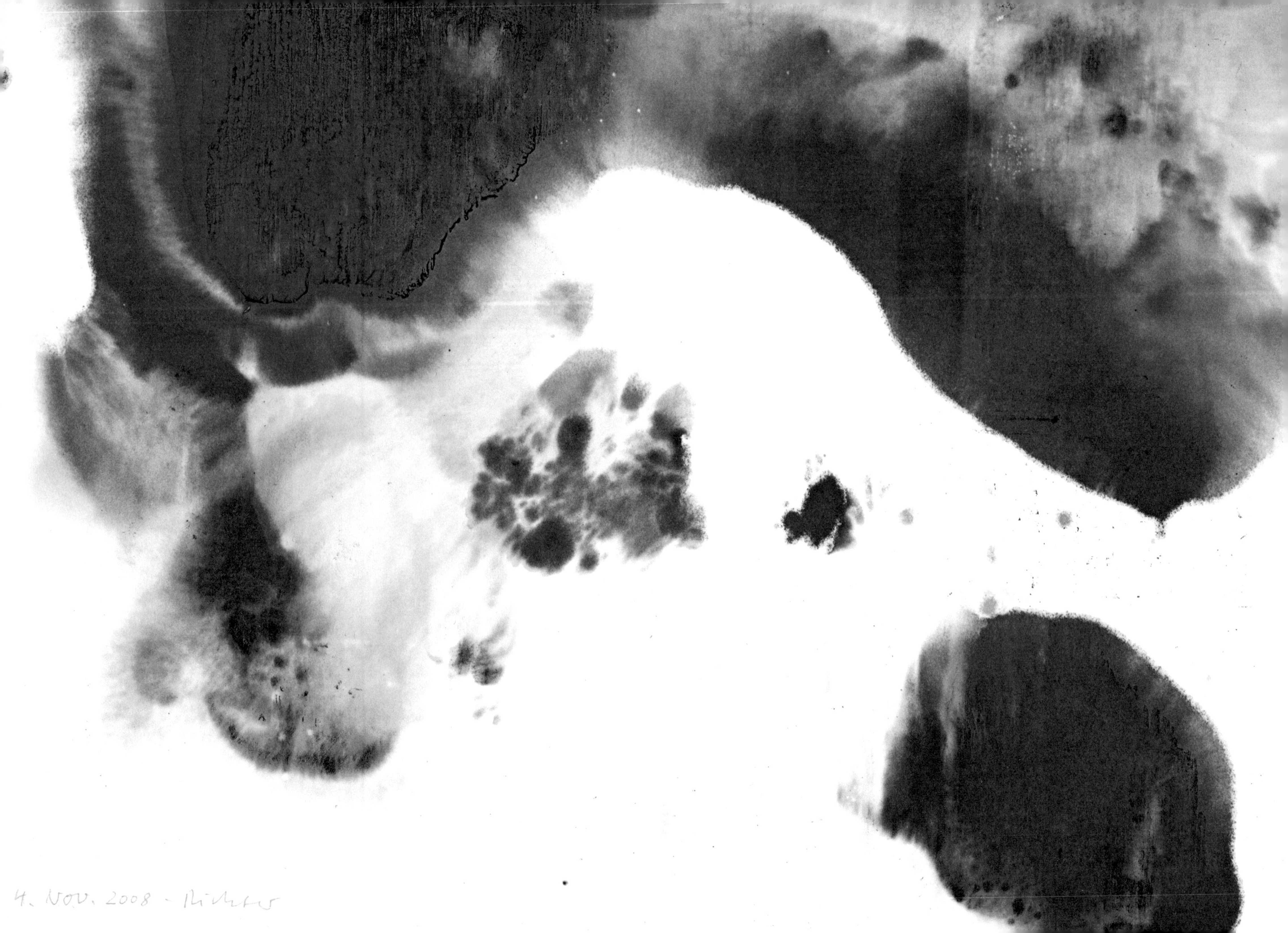
4. Nov. 2008 · Richter

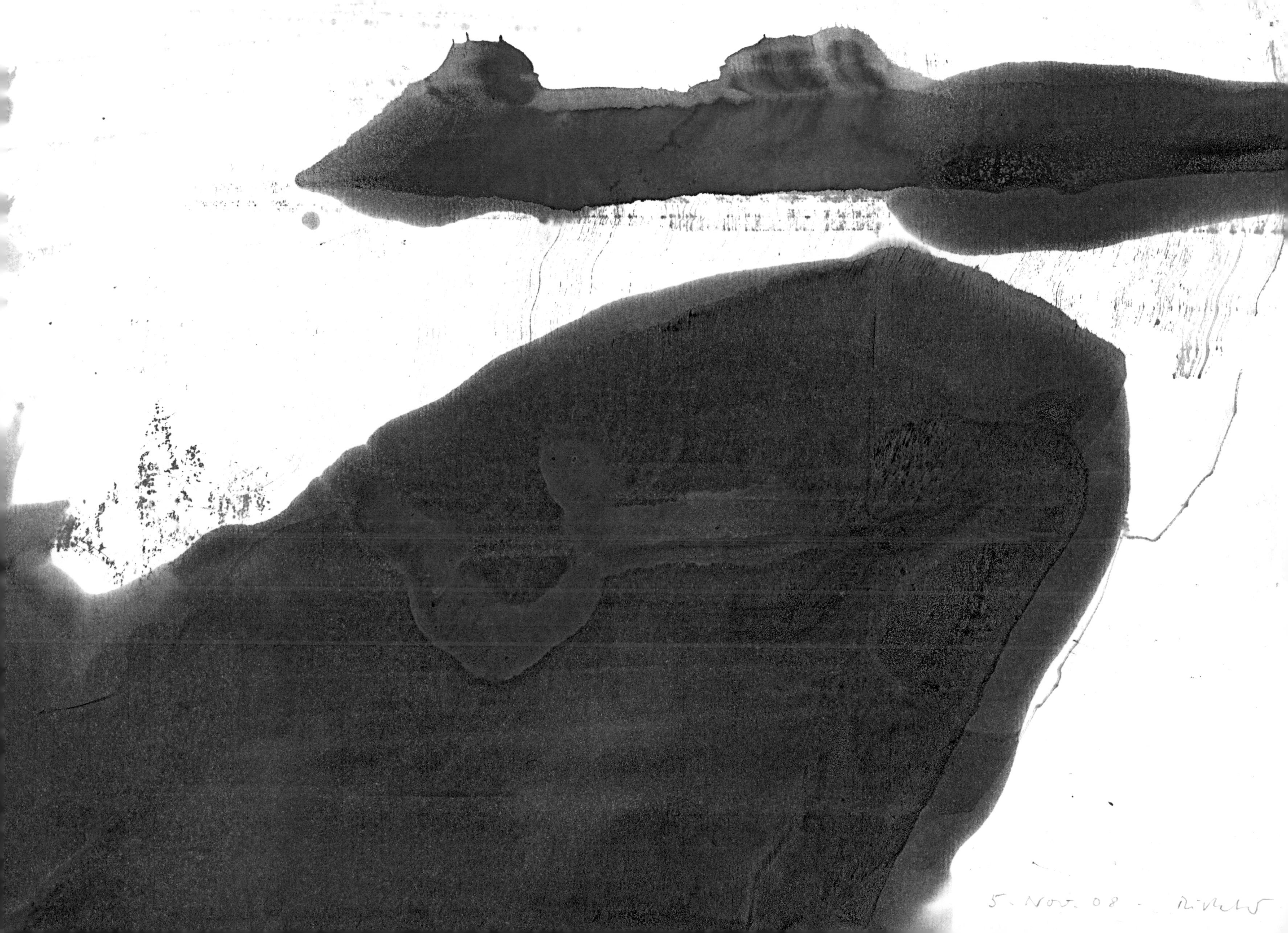
5. Nov. 08

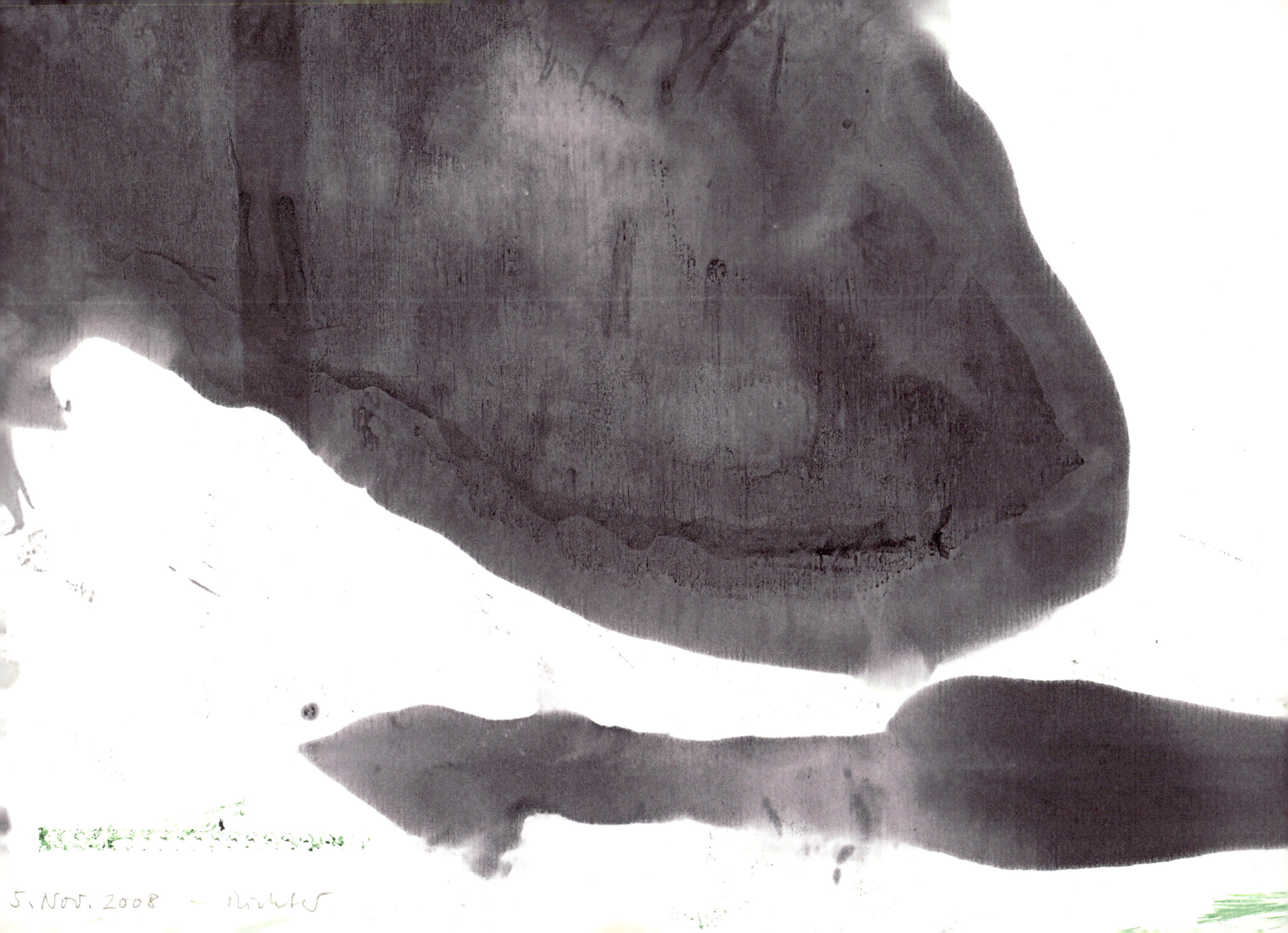
5. Nov. 2008 – Richter

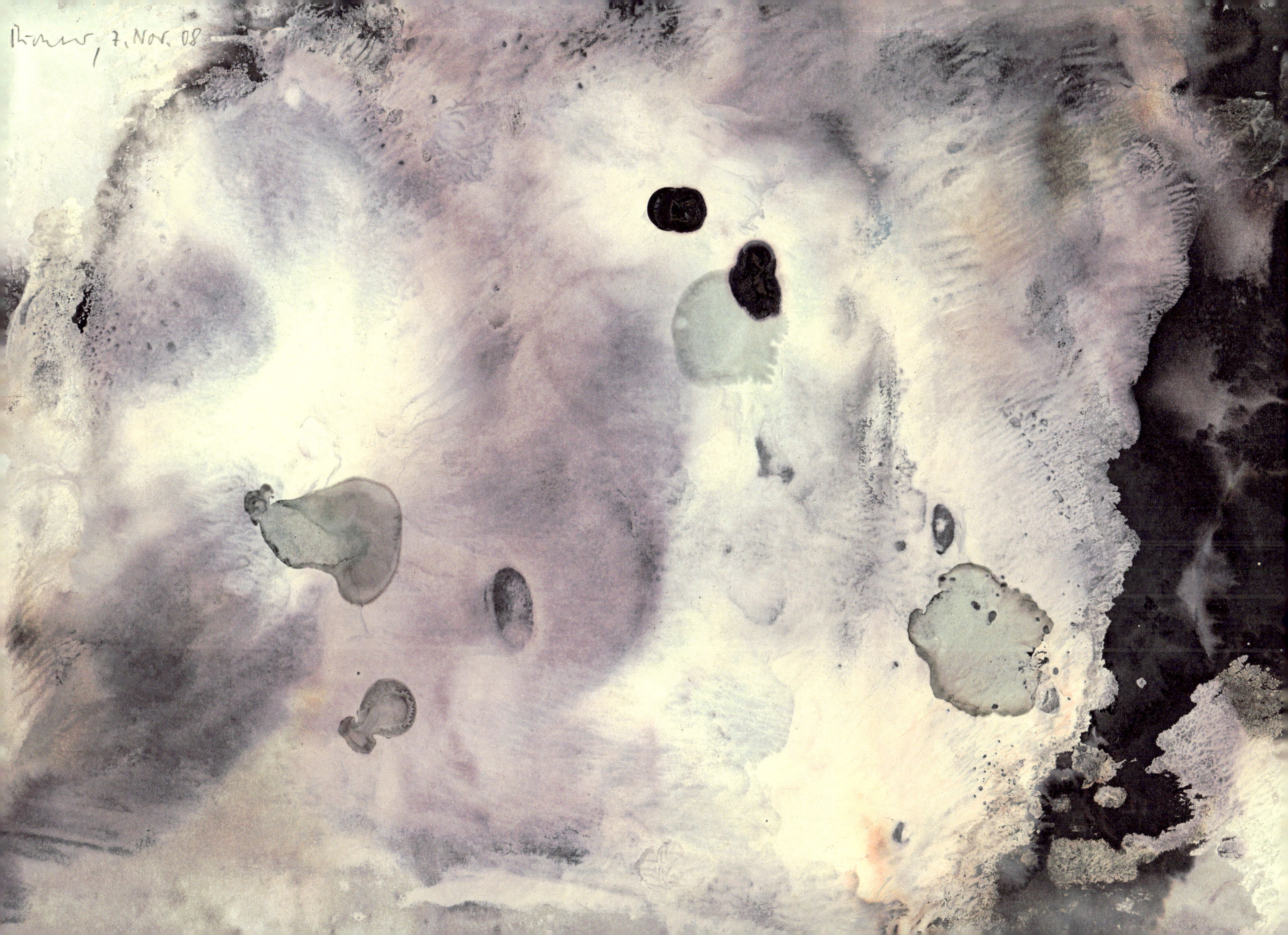
7. Nov. 08

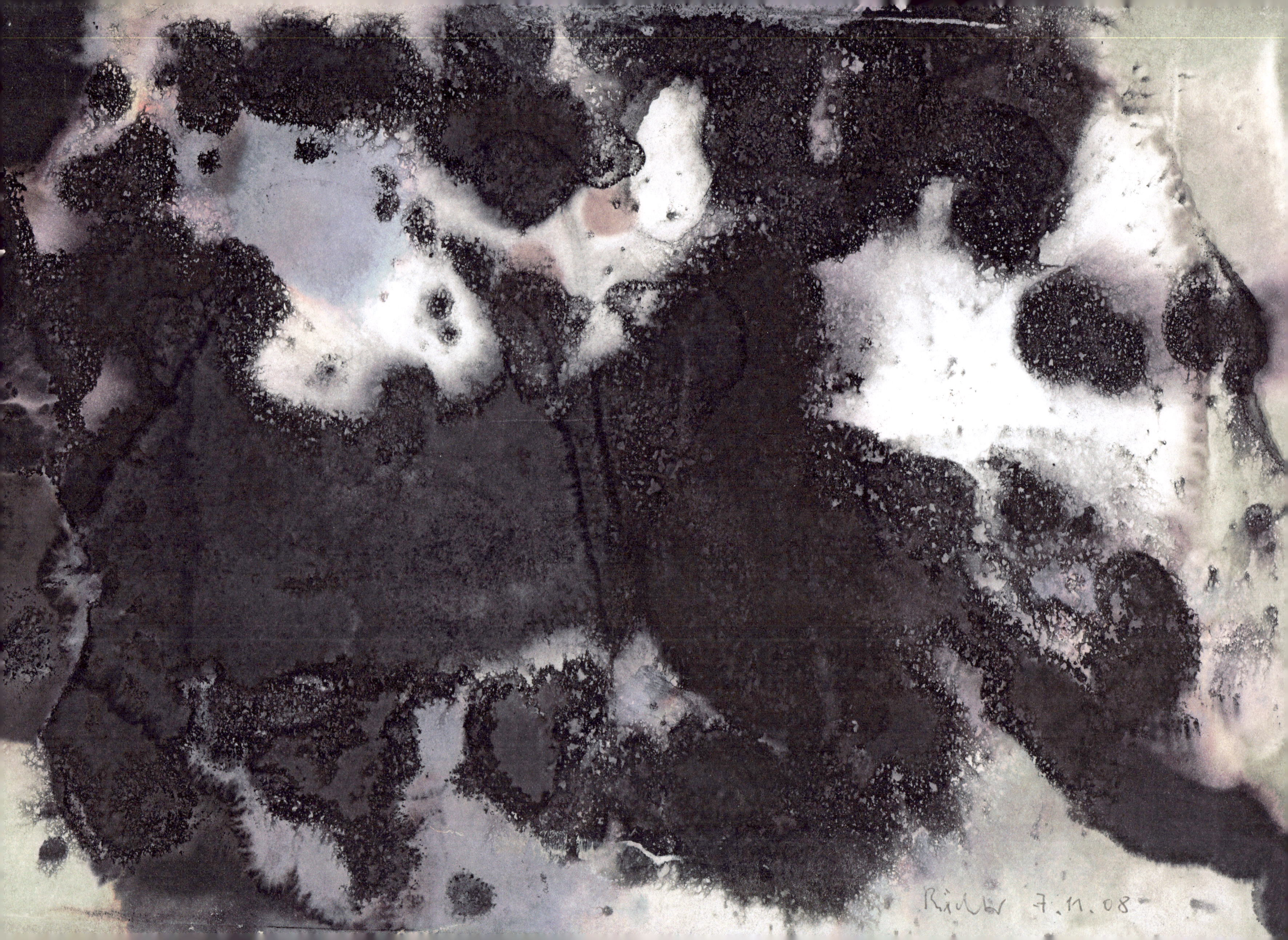
Richter 7.11.08

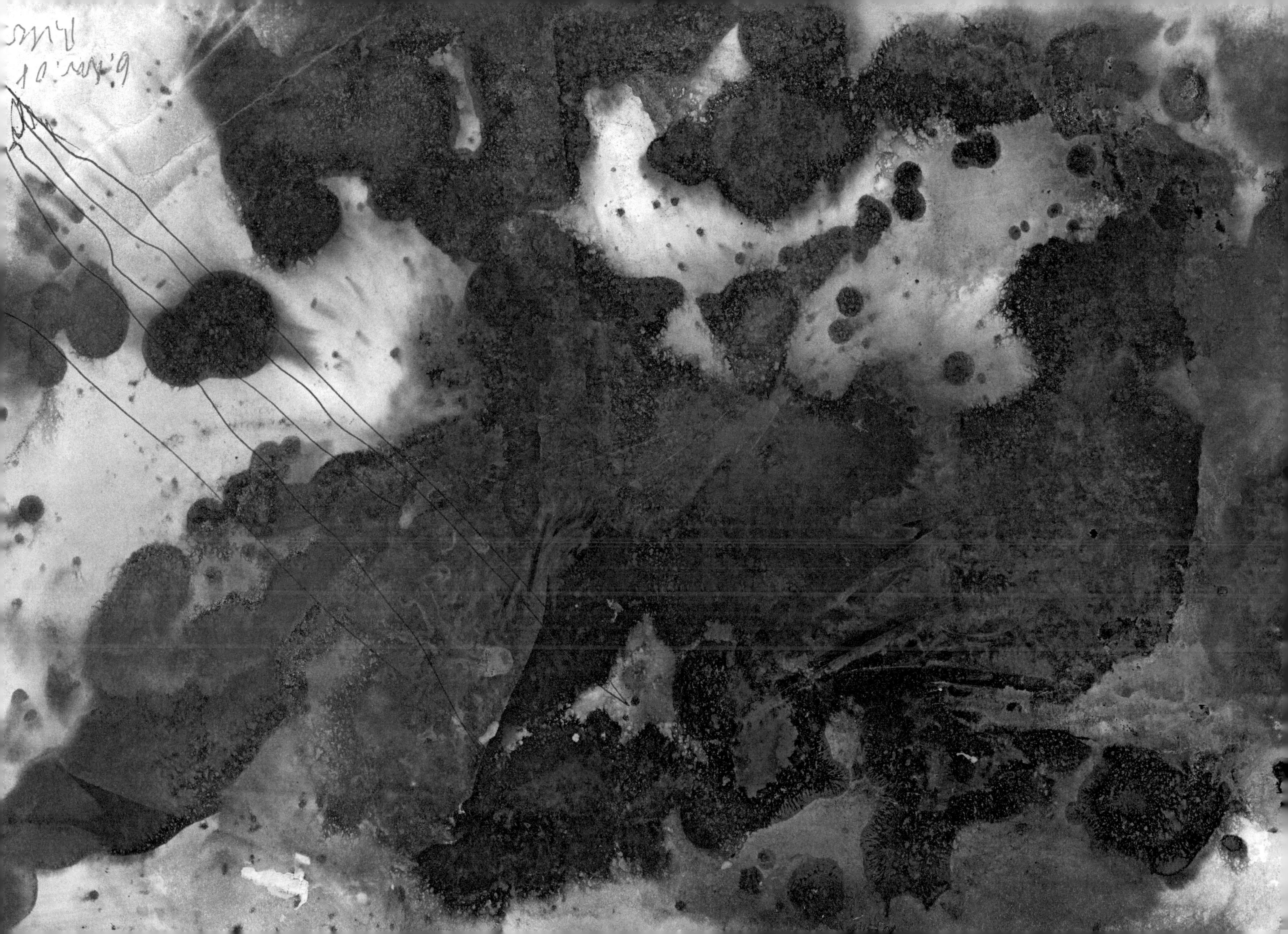

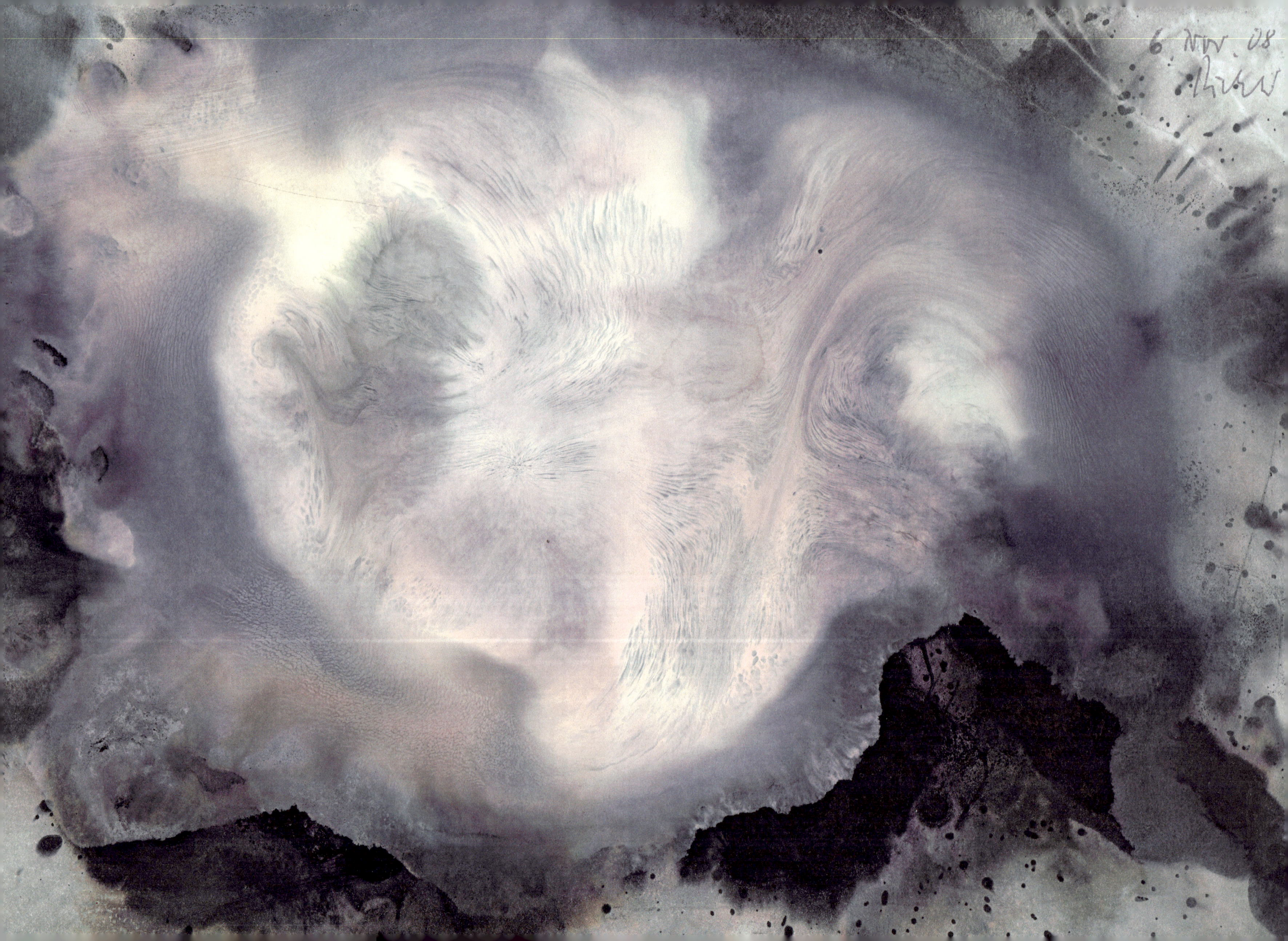
6 Nov 08

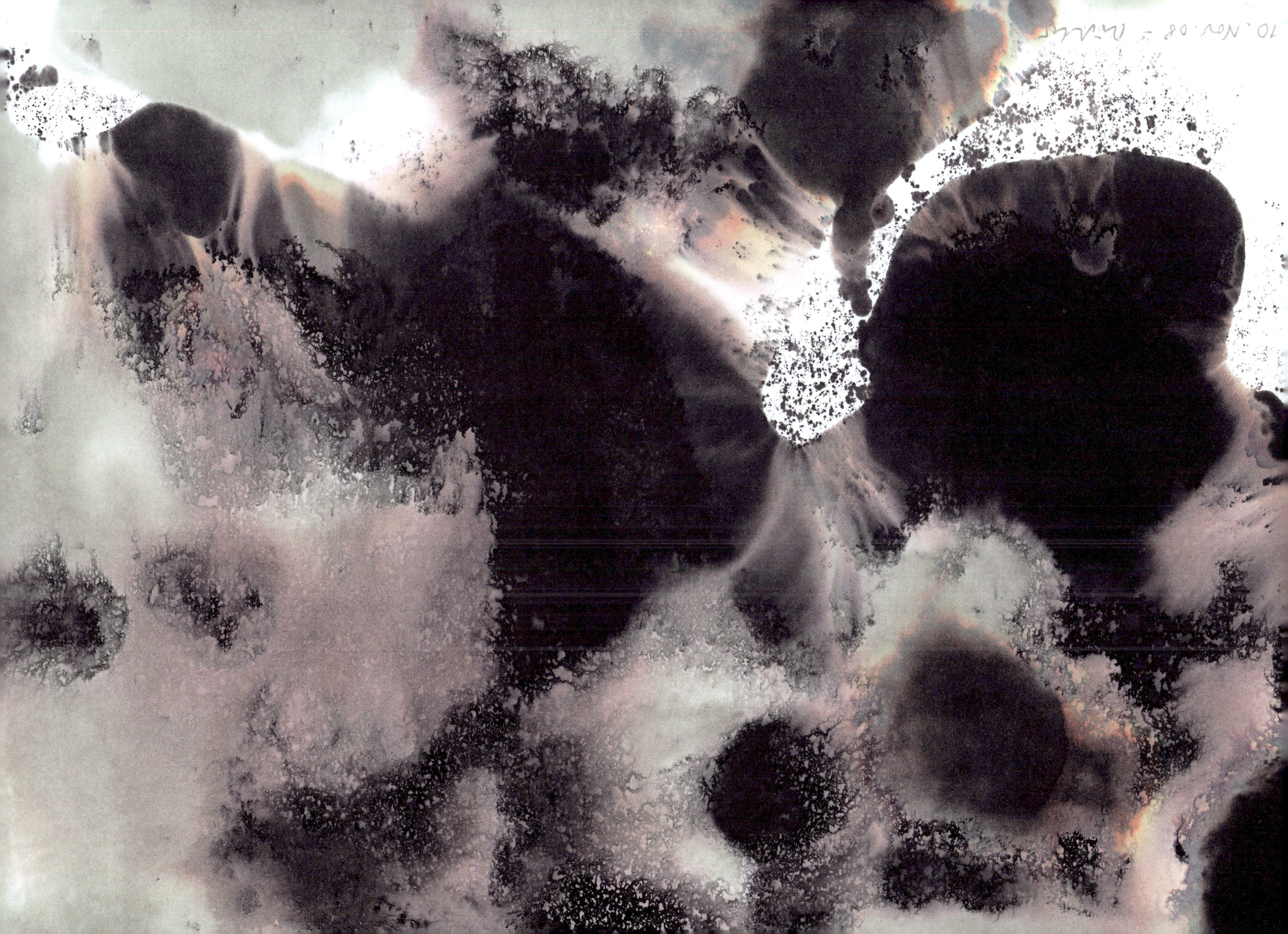

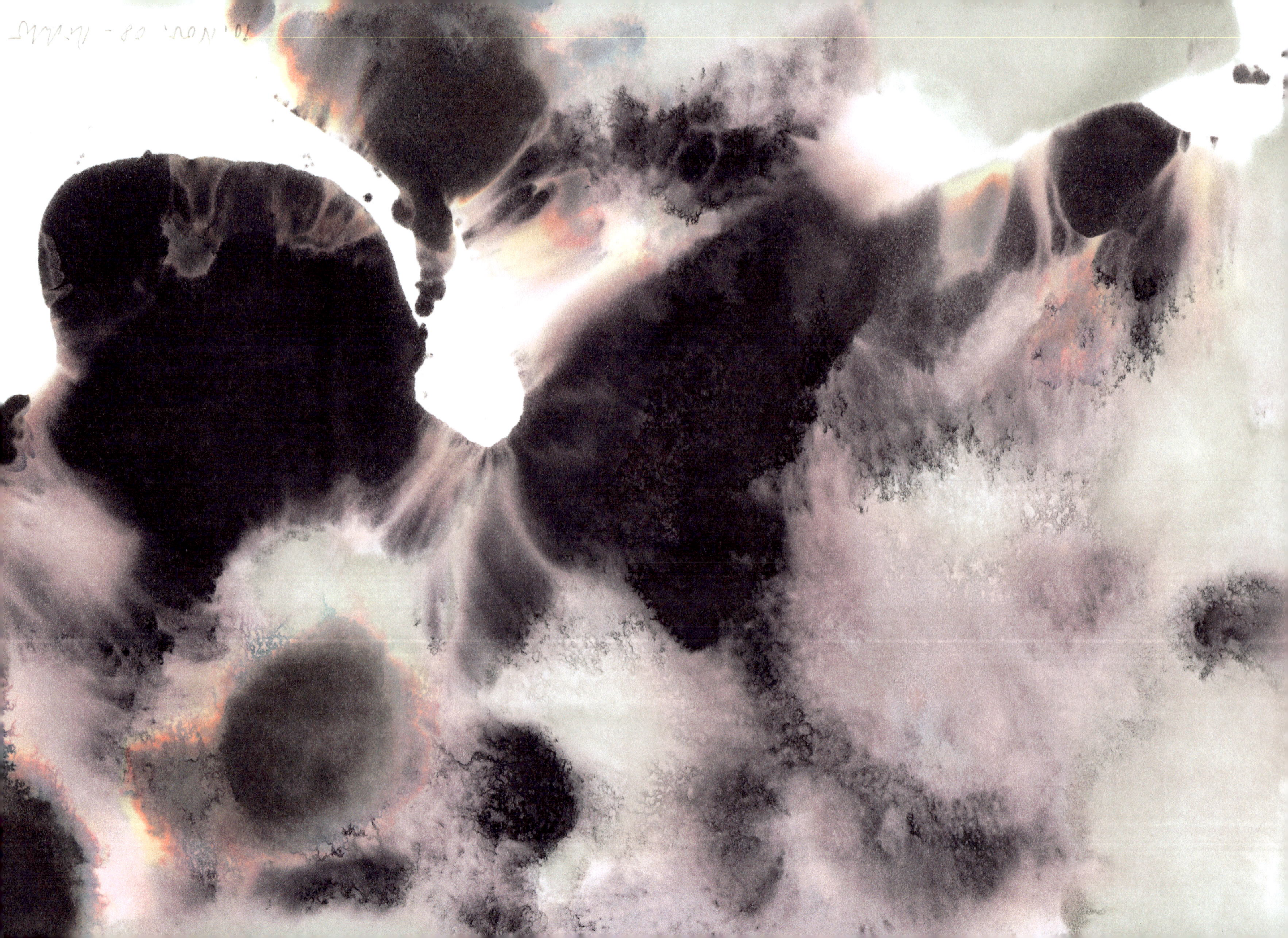

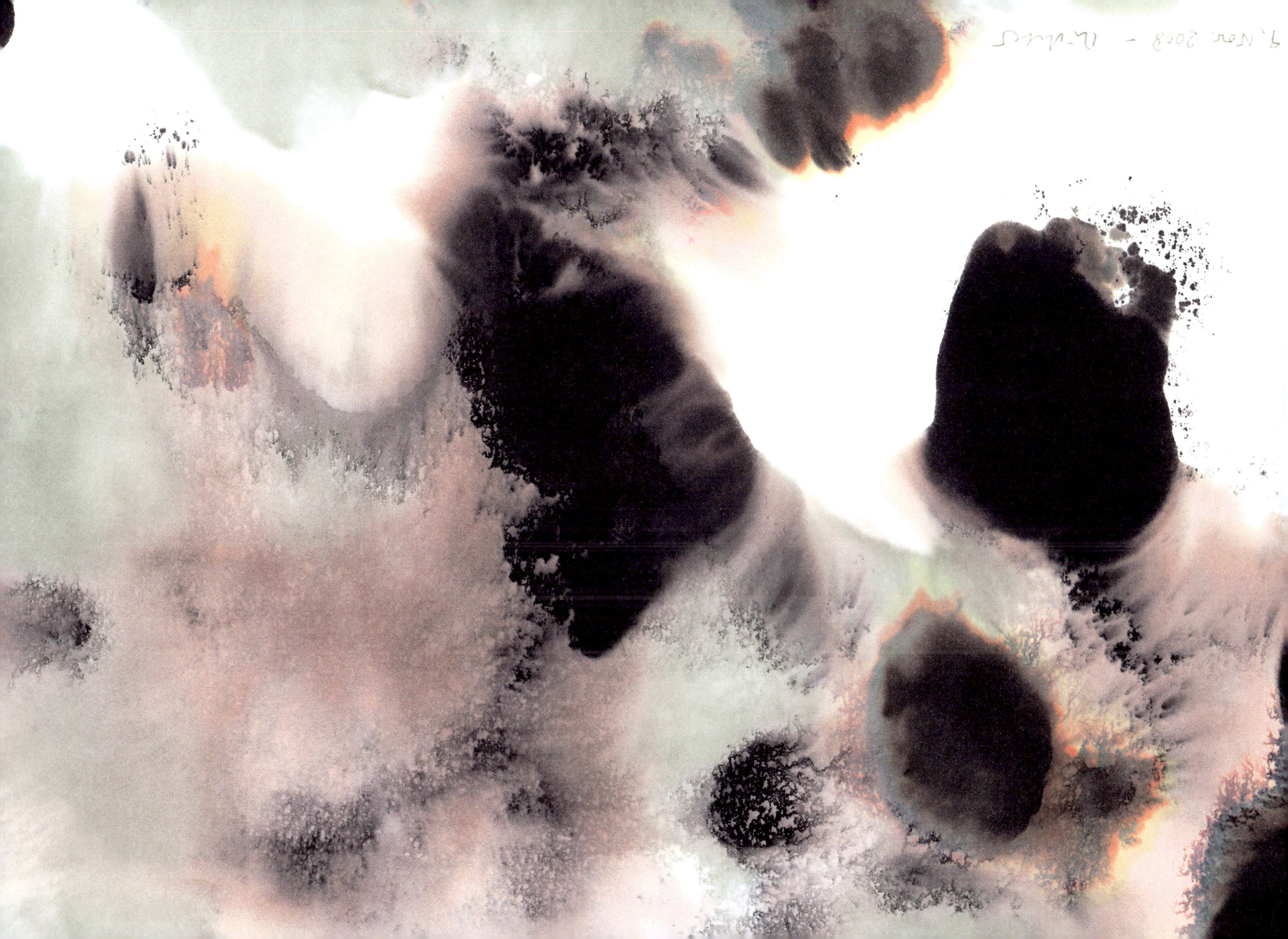

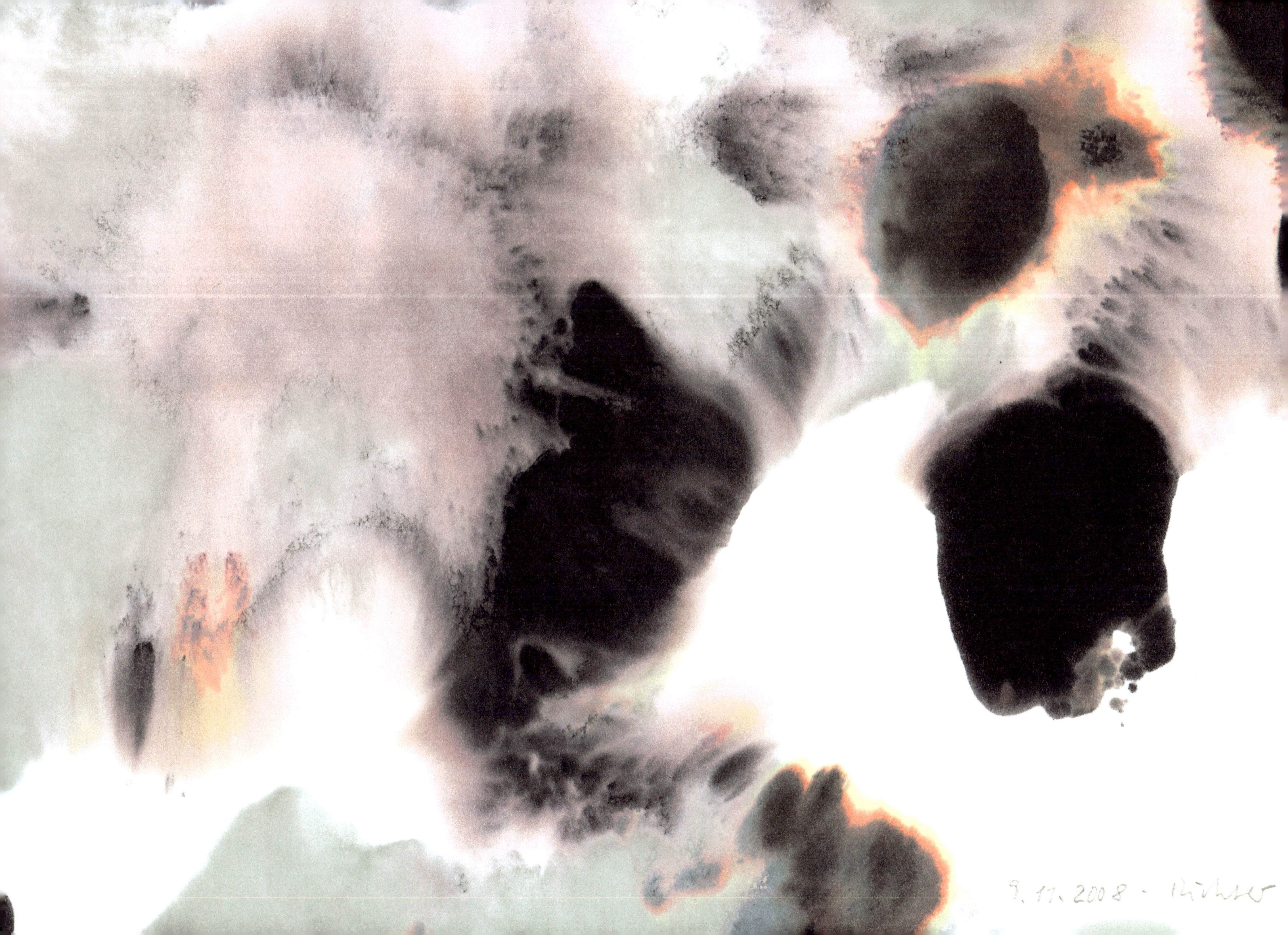
9. 11. 2008 · Richter

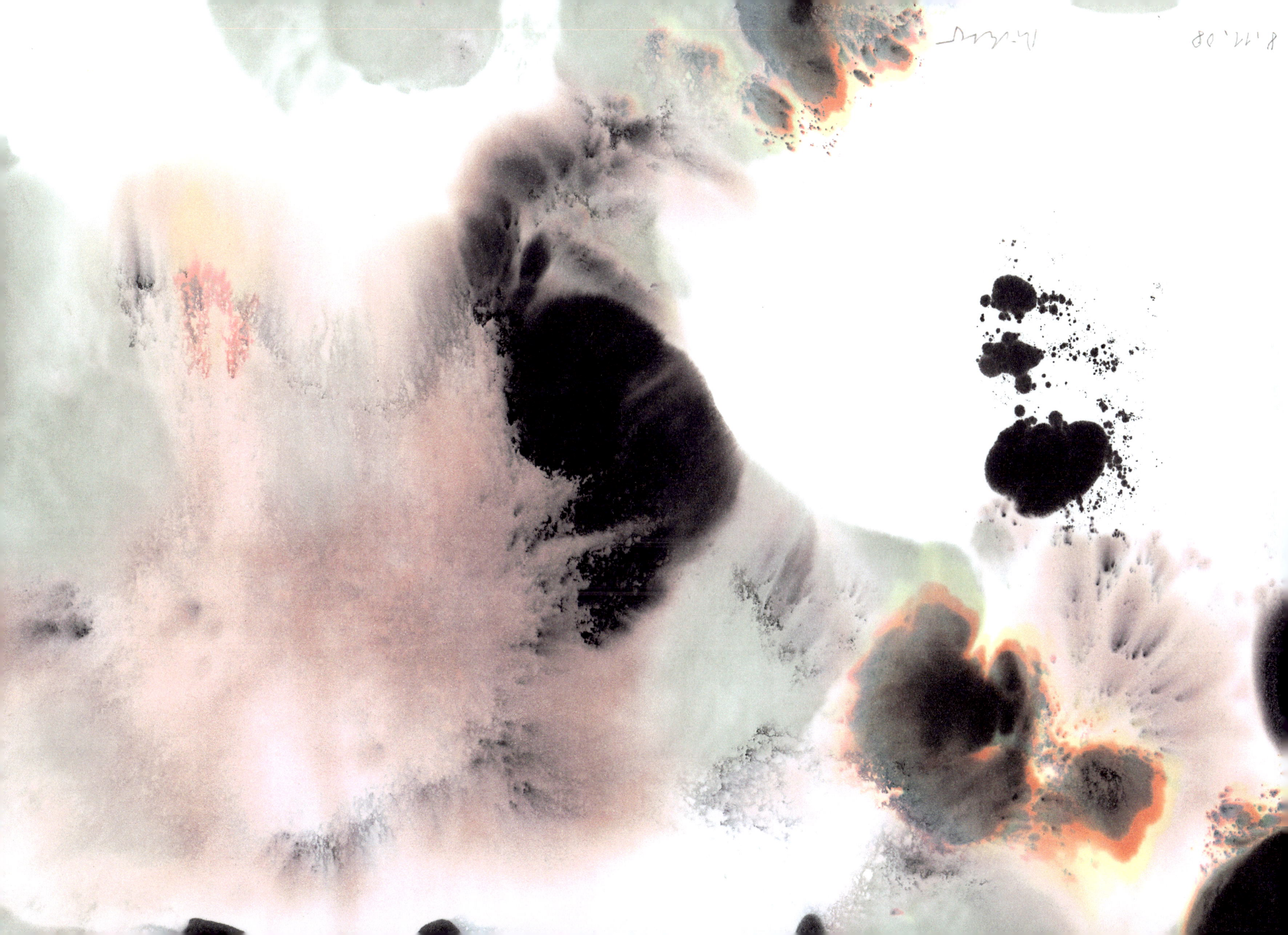

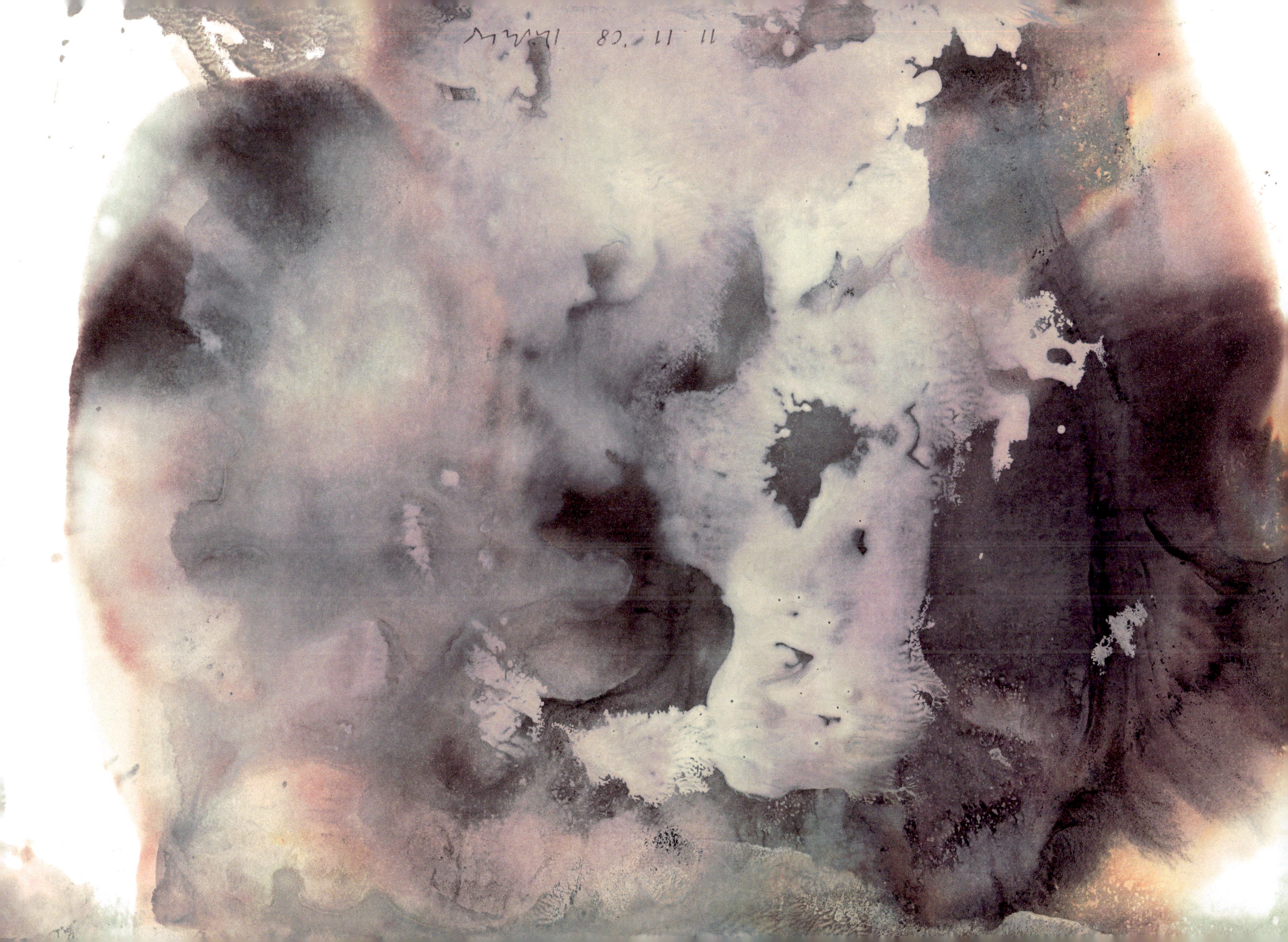

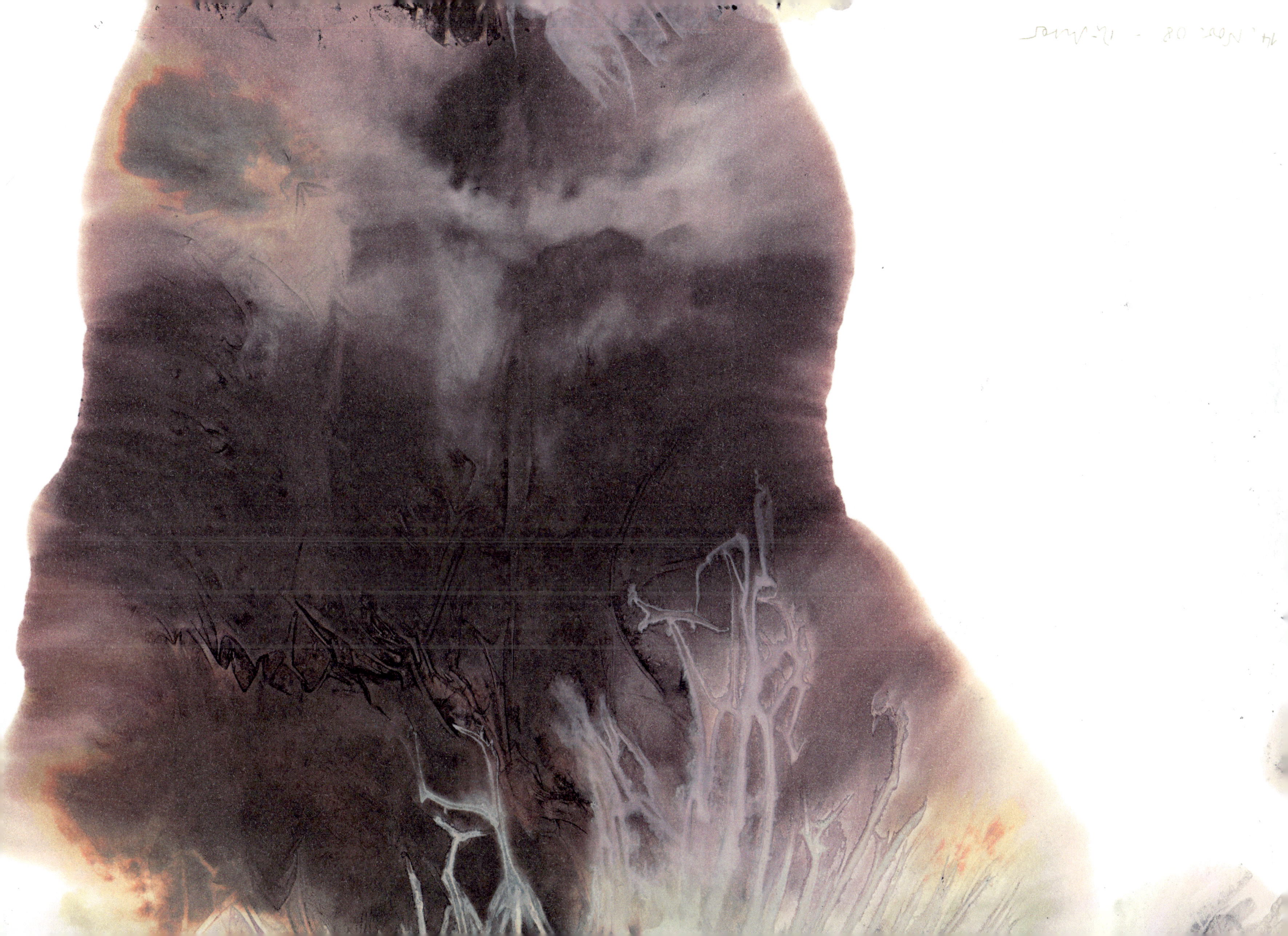

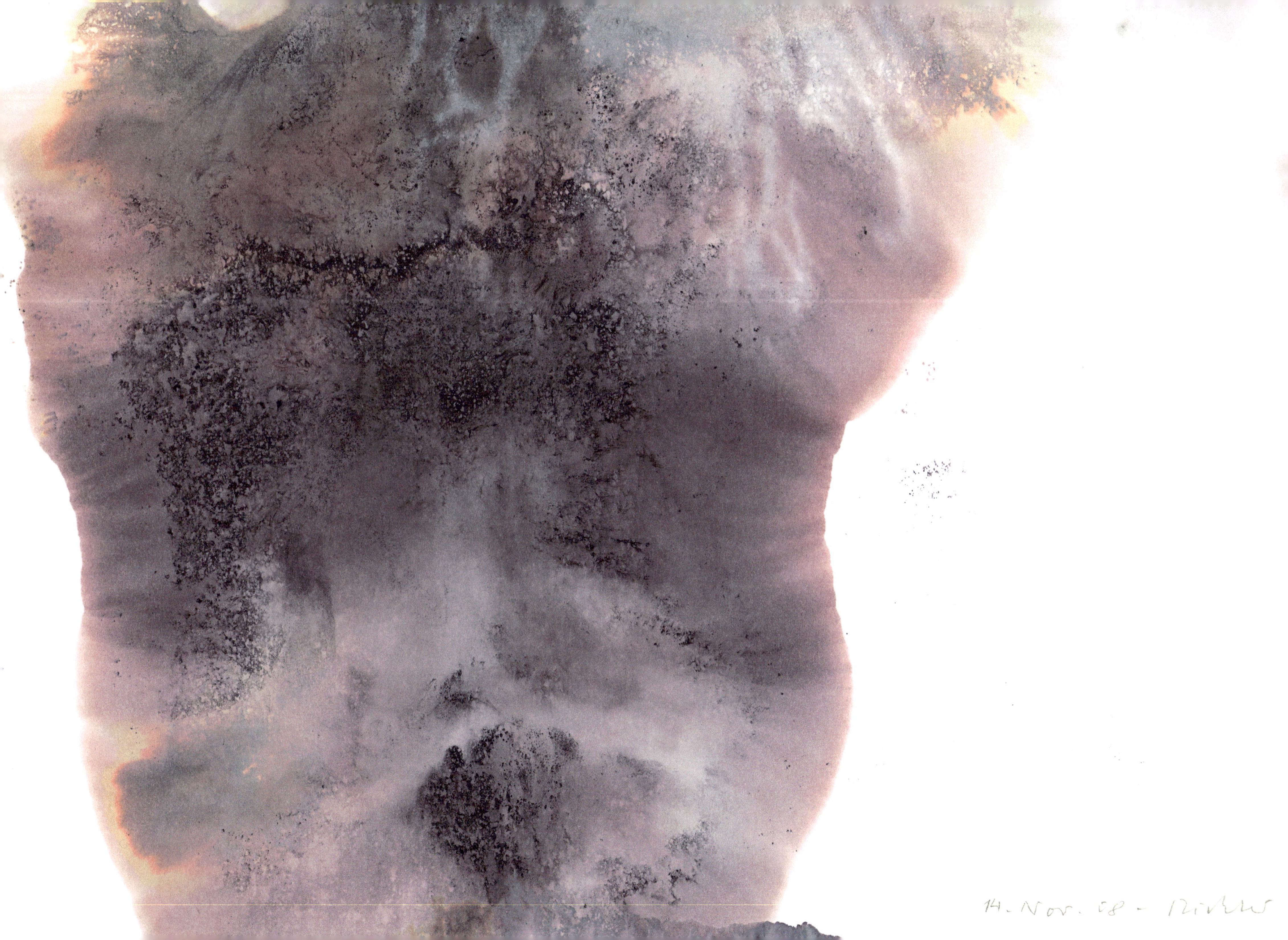
14. Nov. 08 - Richter

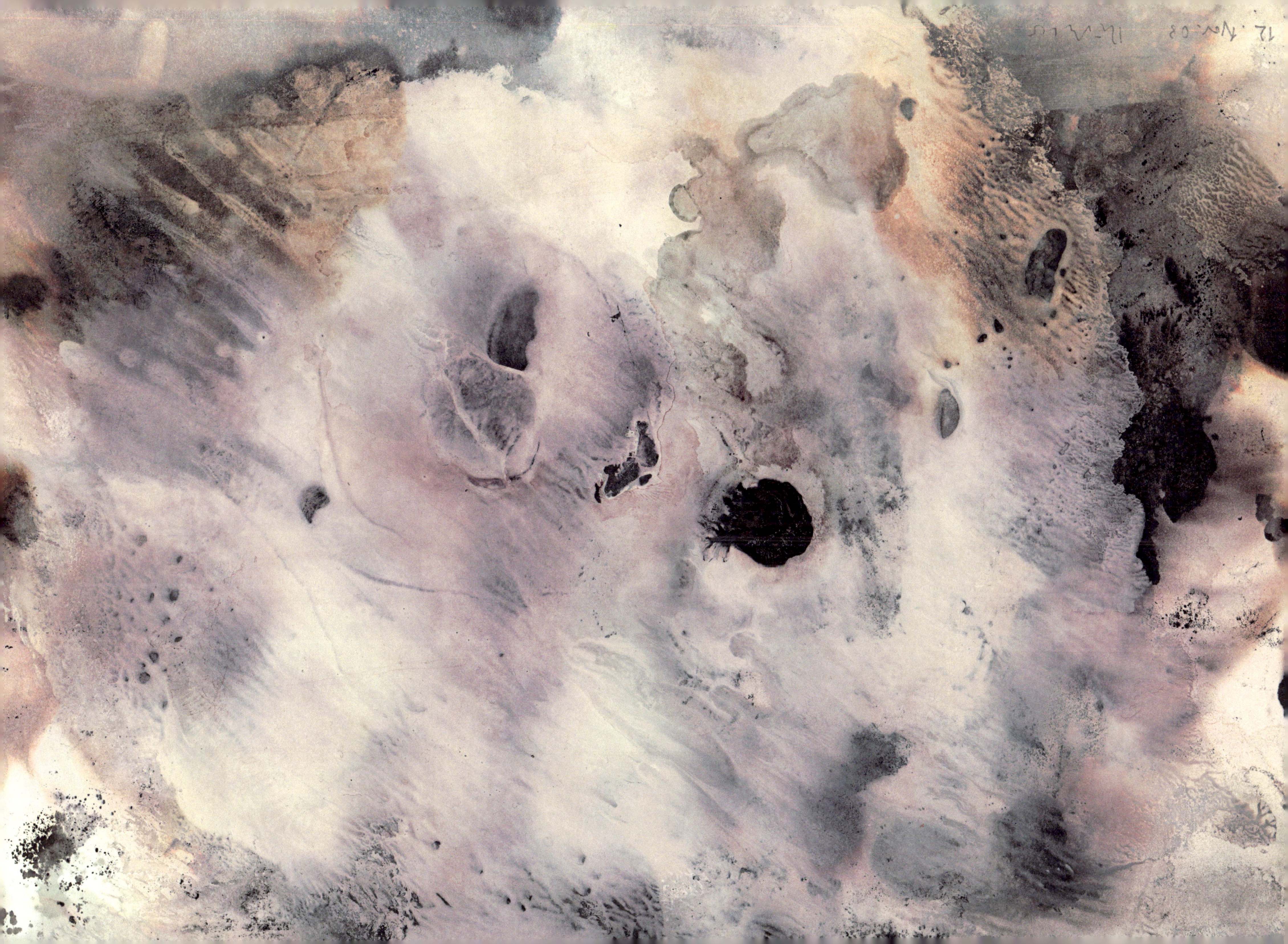

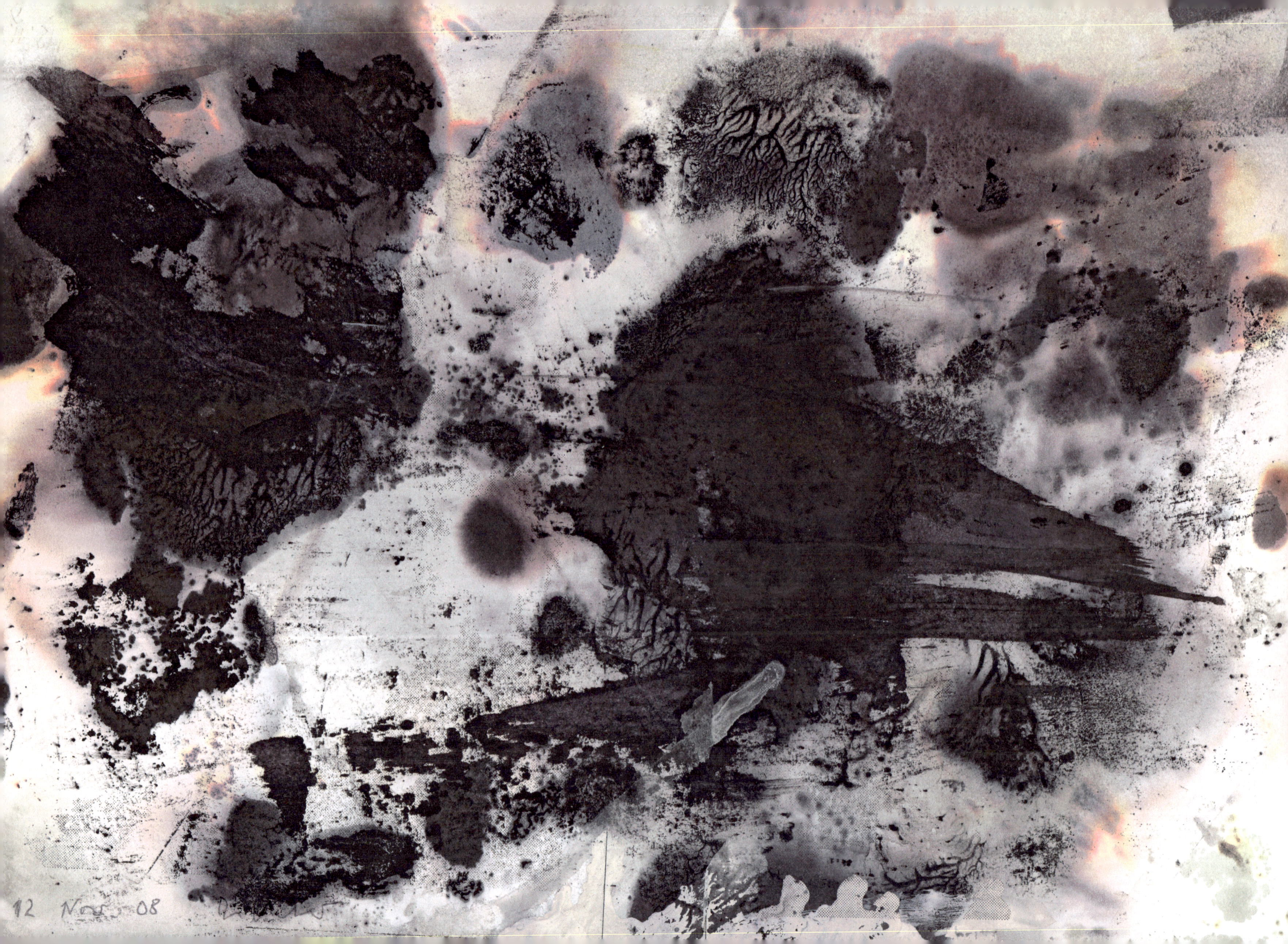
12 Nov 08

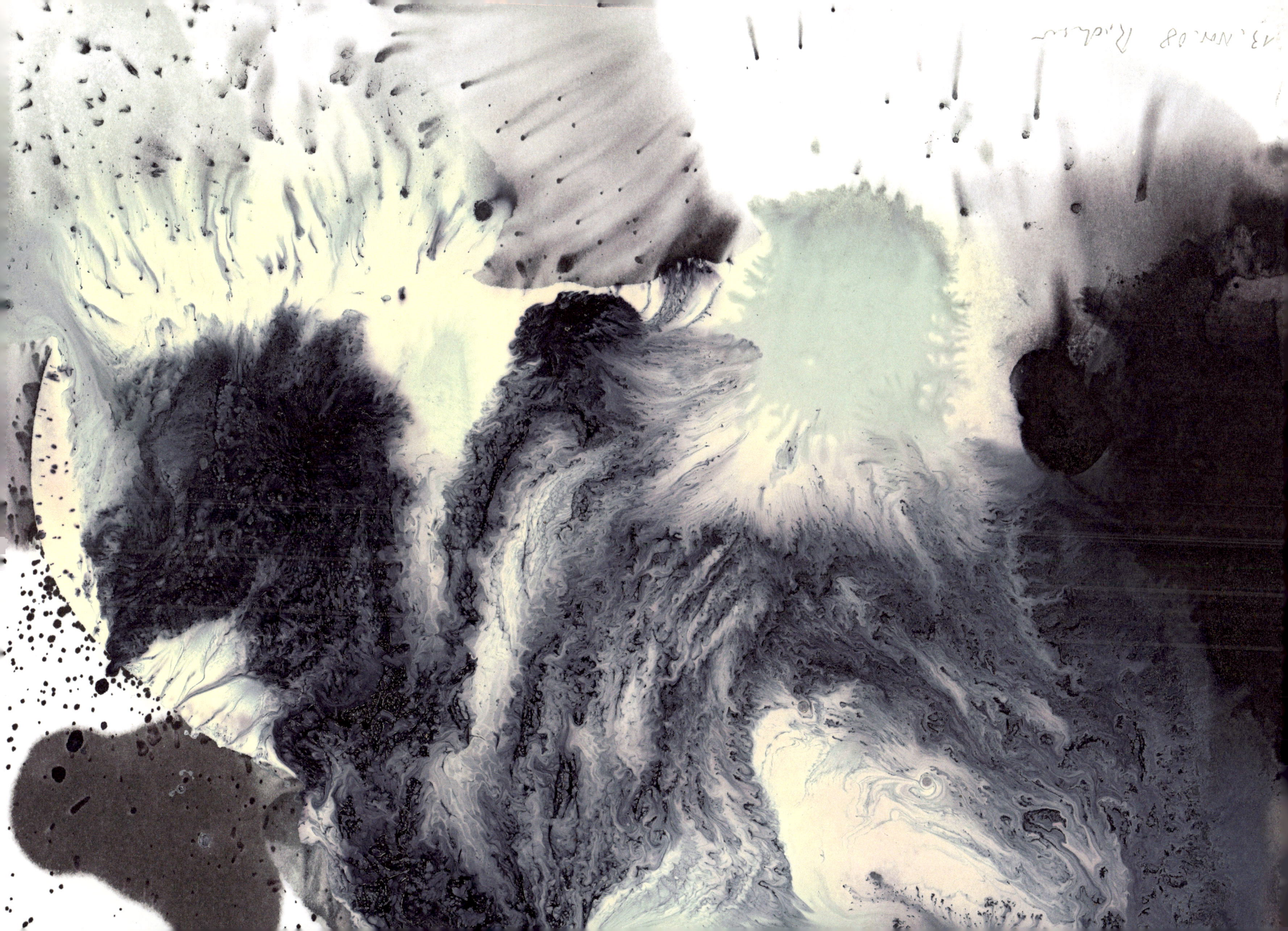

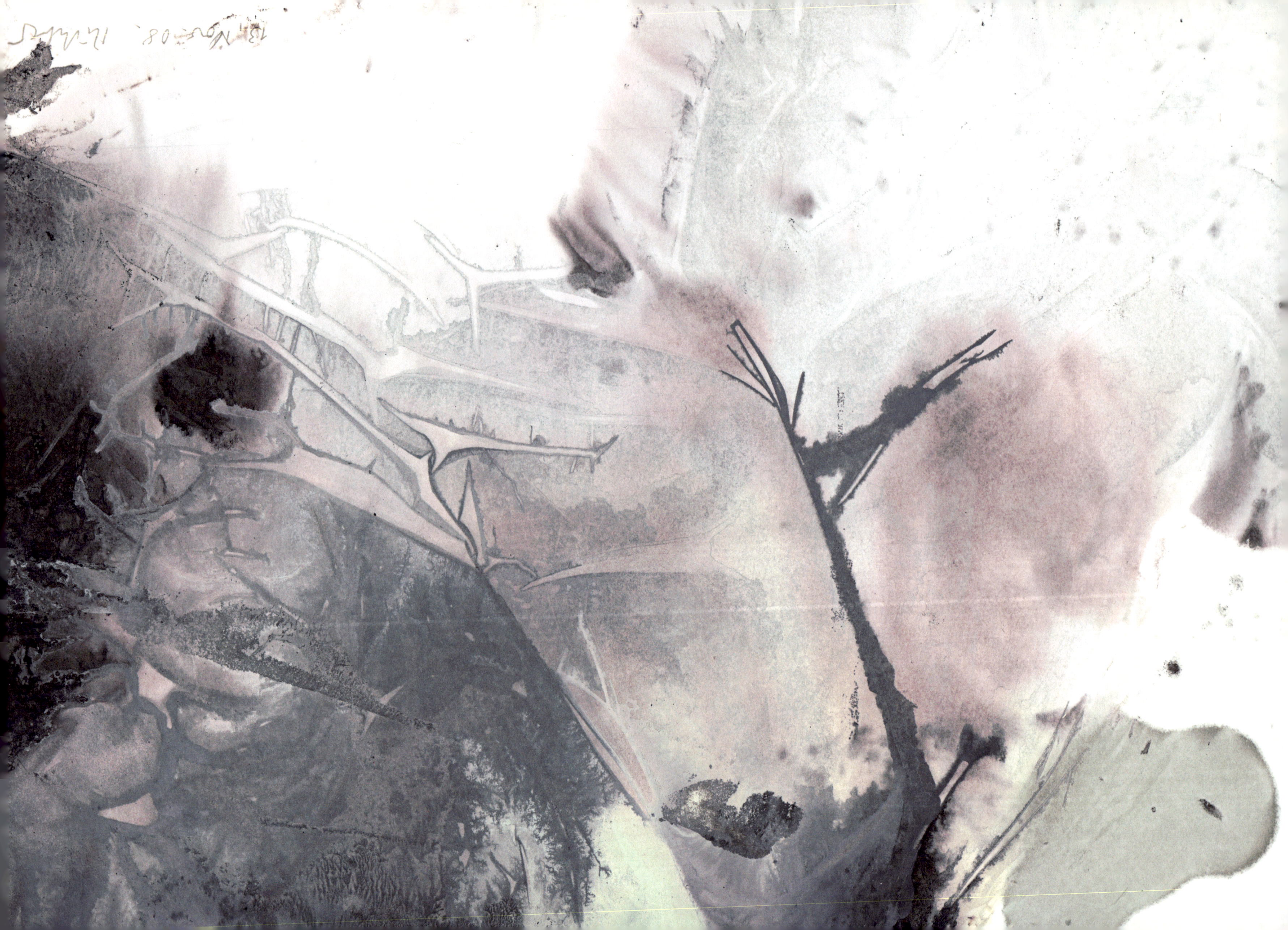

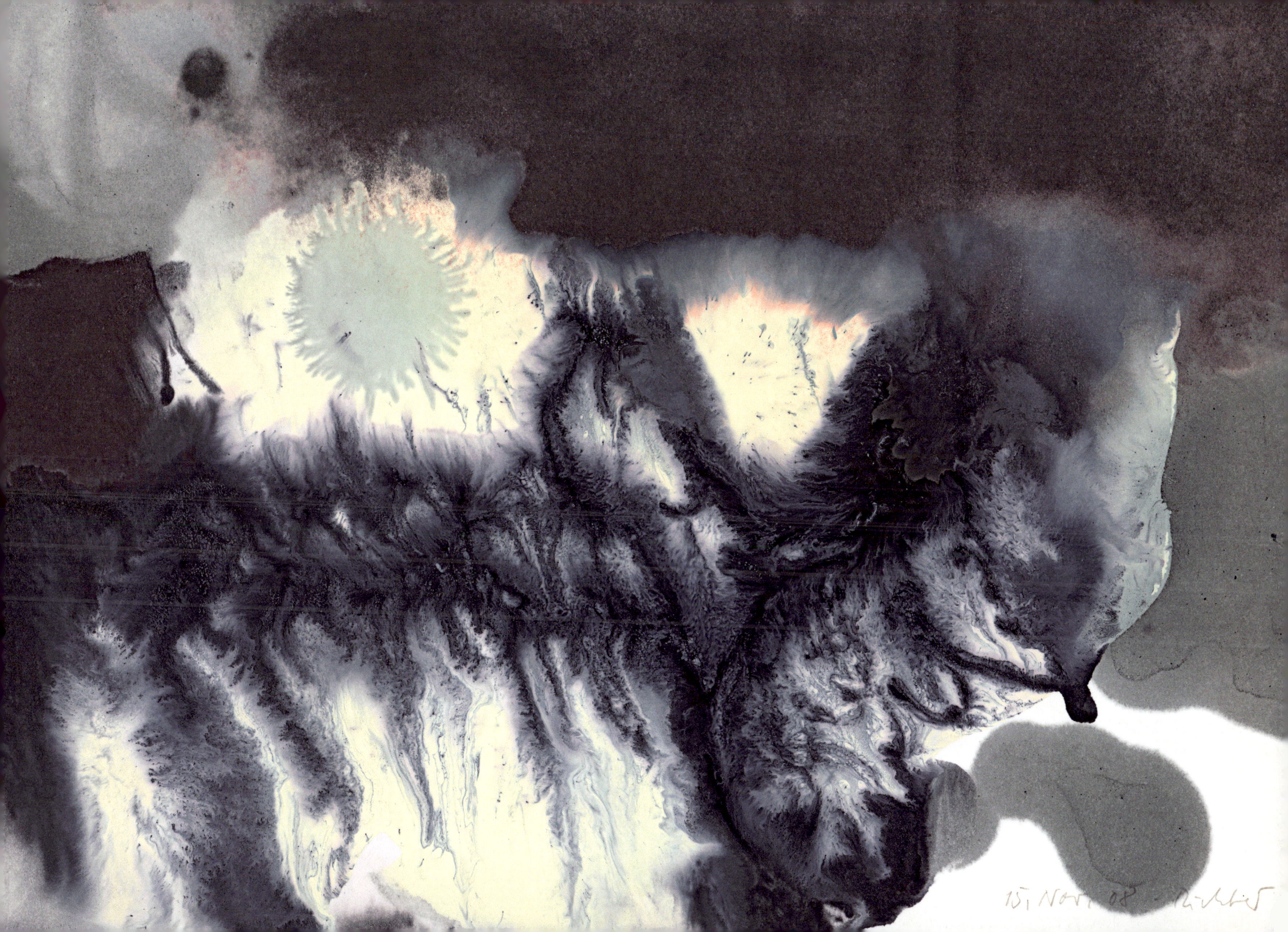
15. Nov. 08

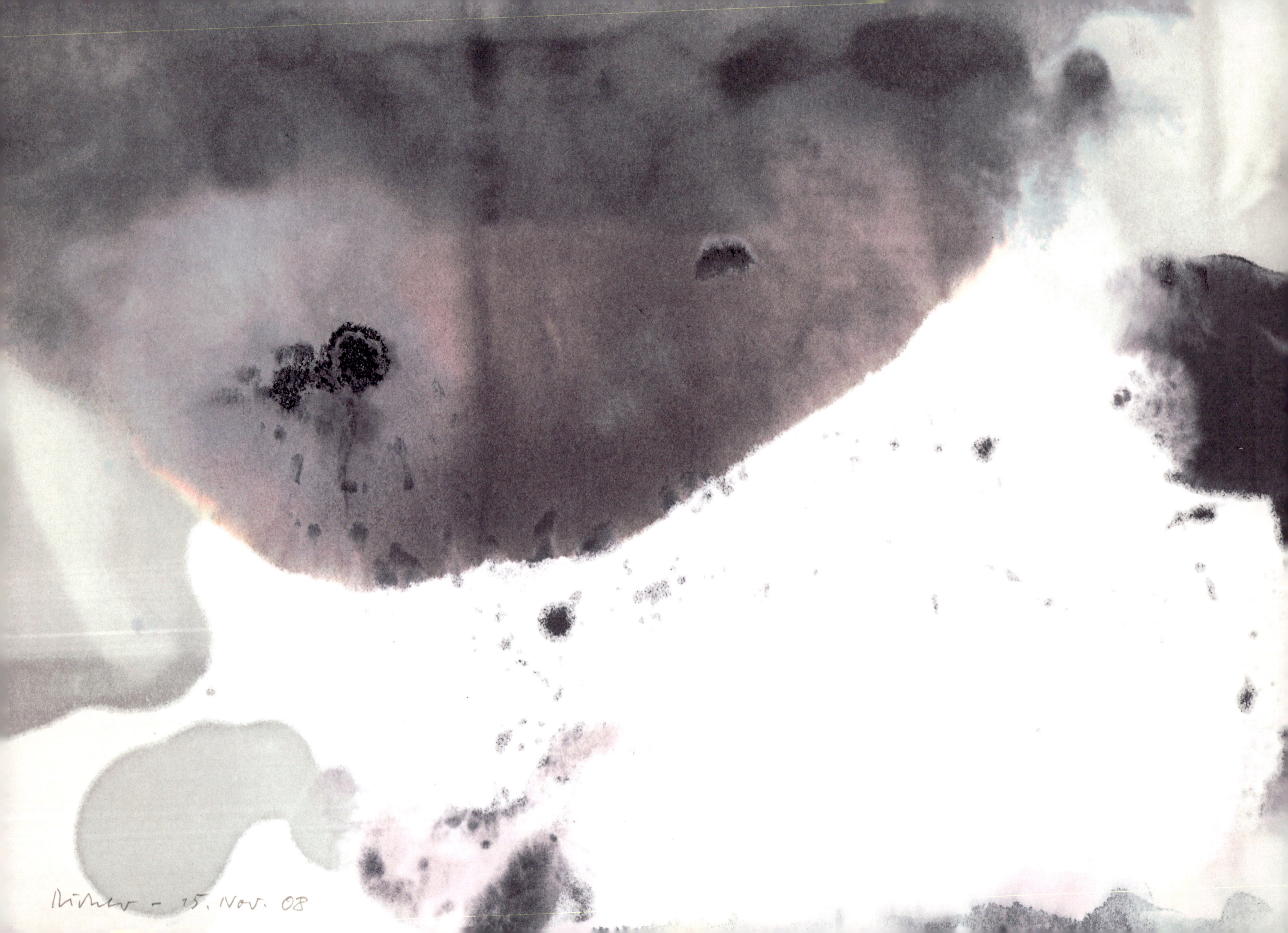
Richter - 15. Nov. 08

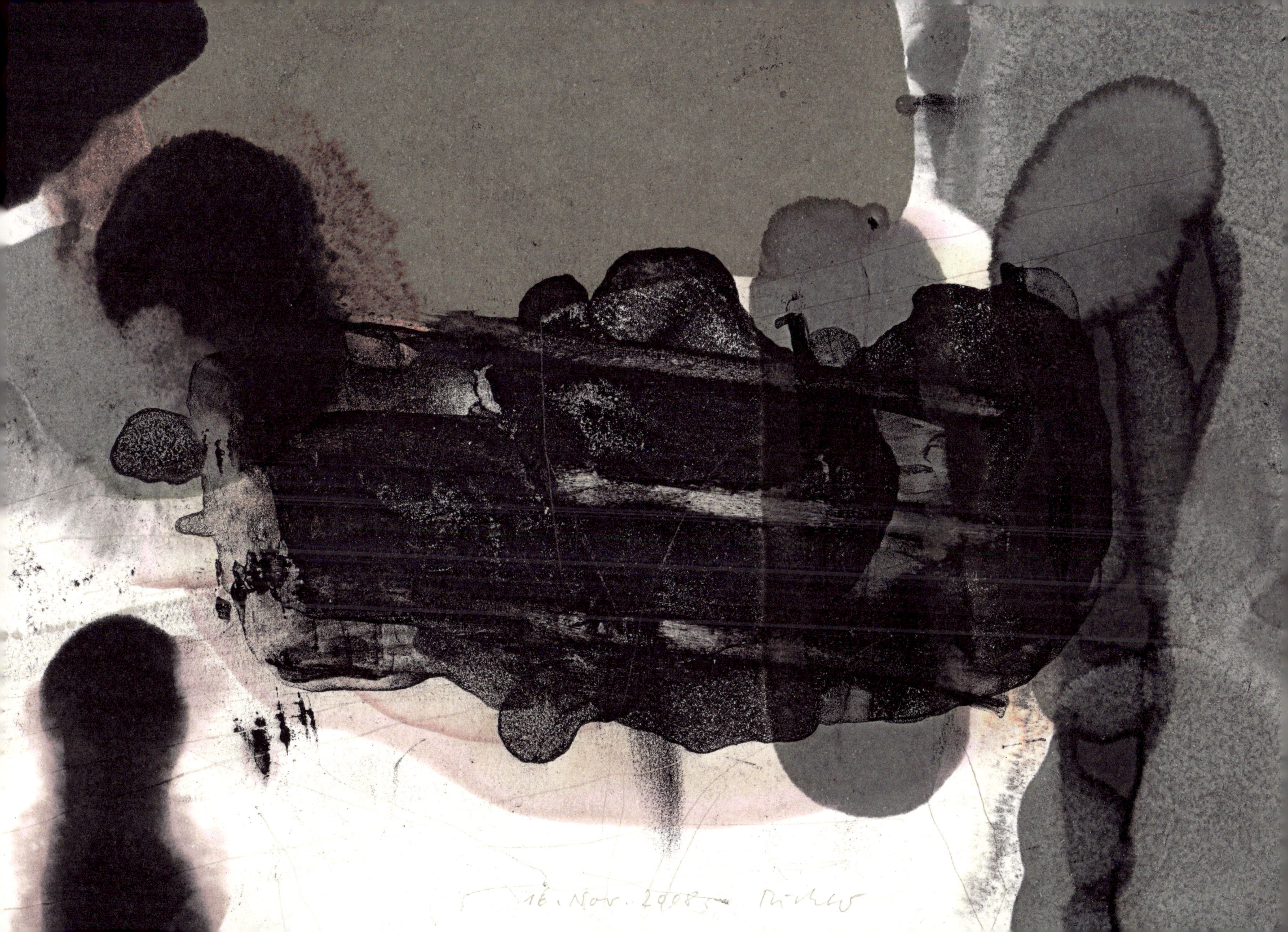
16. Nov. 2008
Richter

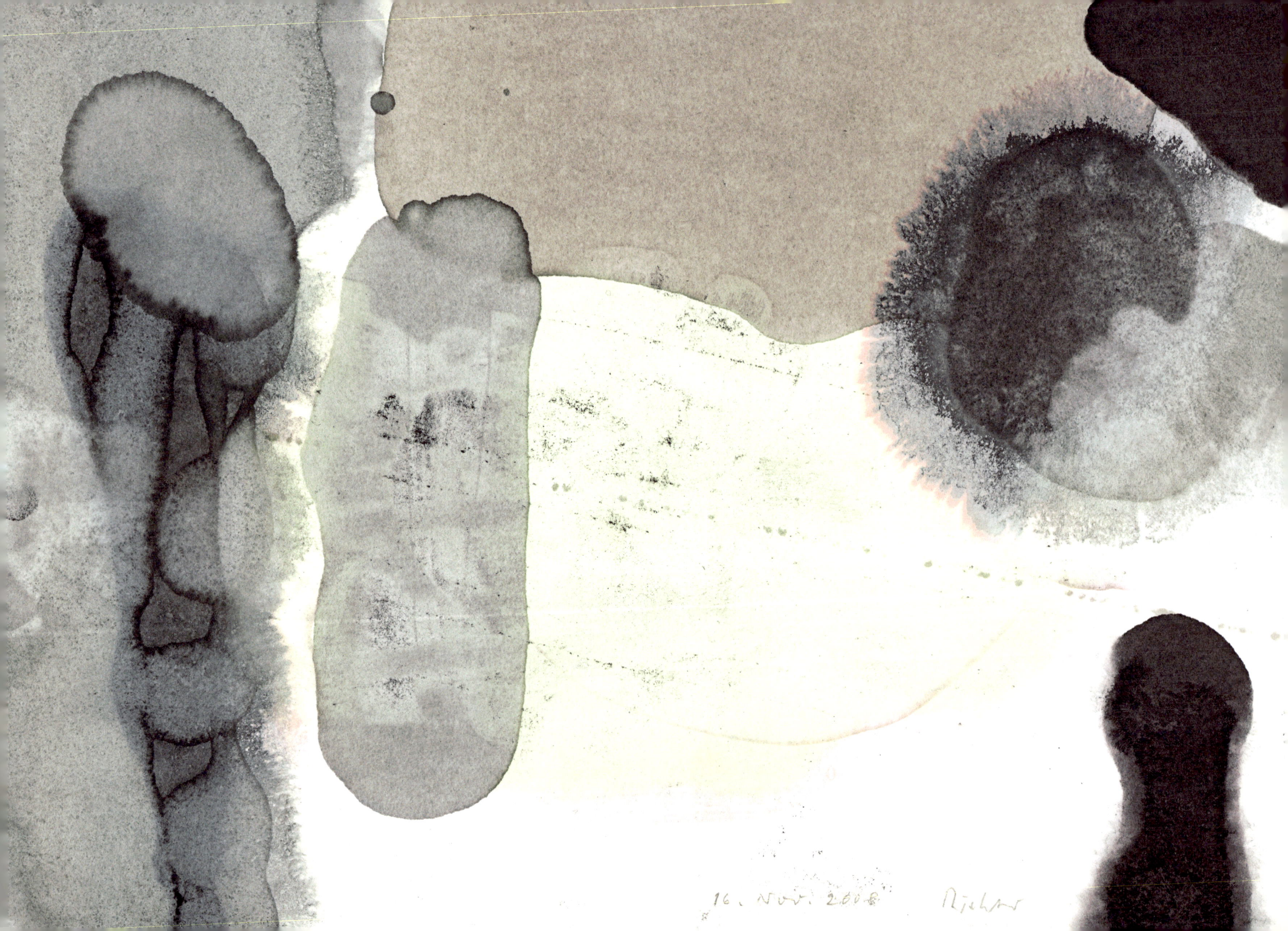
16. Nov. 2008

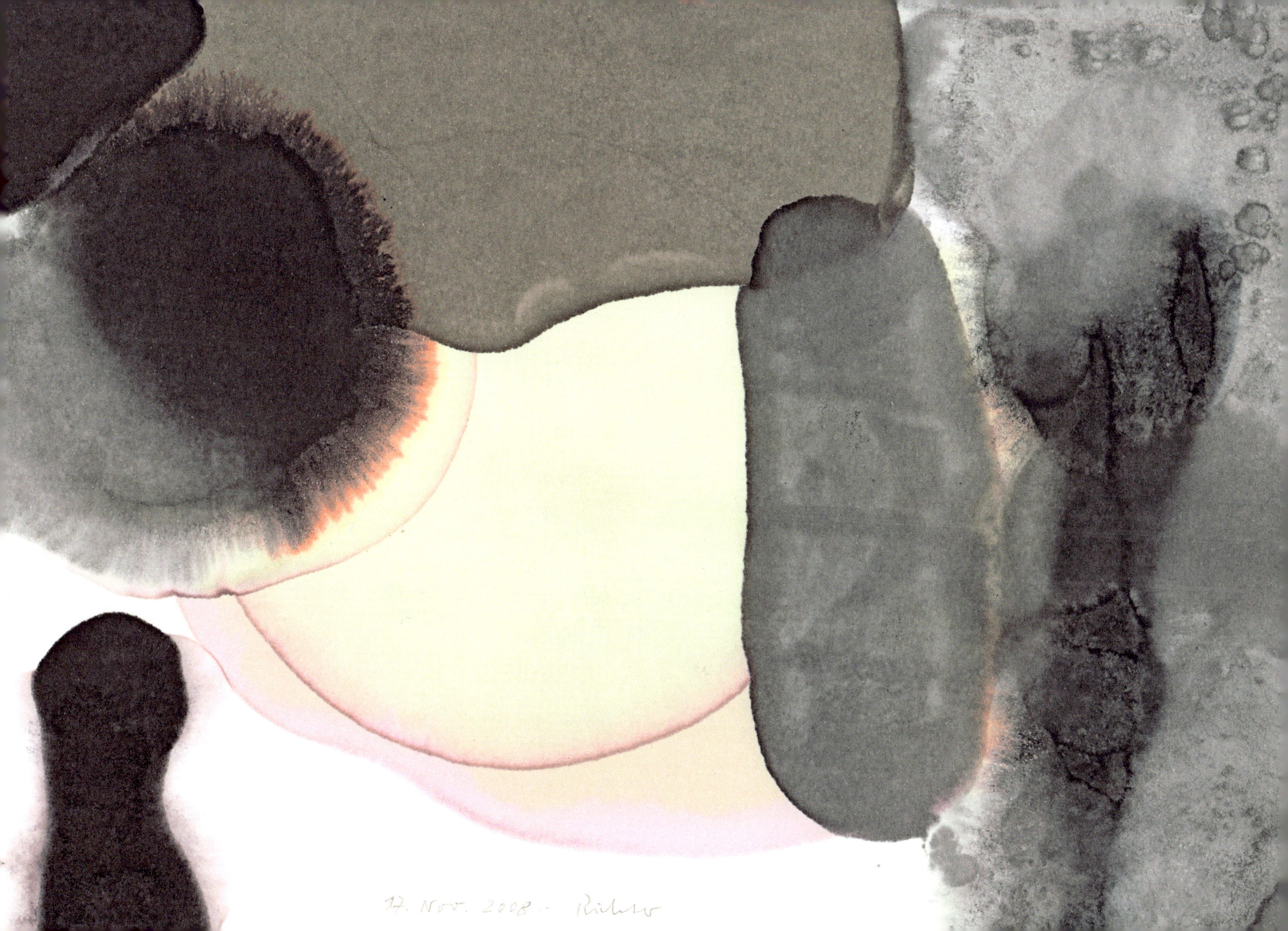
17. Nov. 2008 - Richter

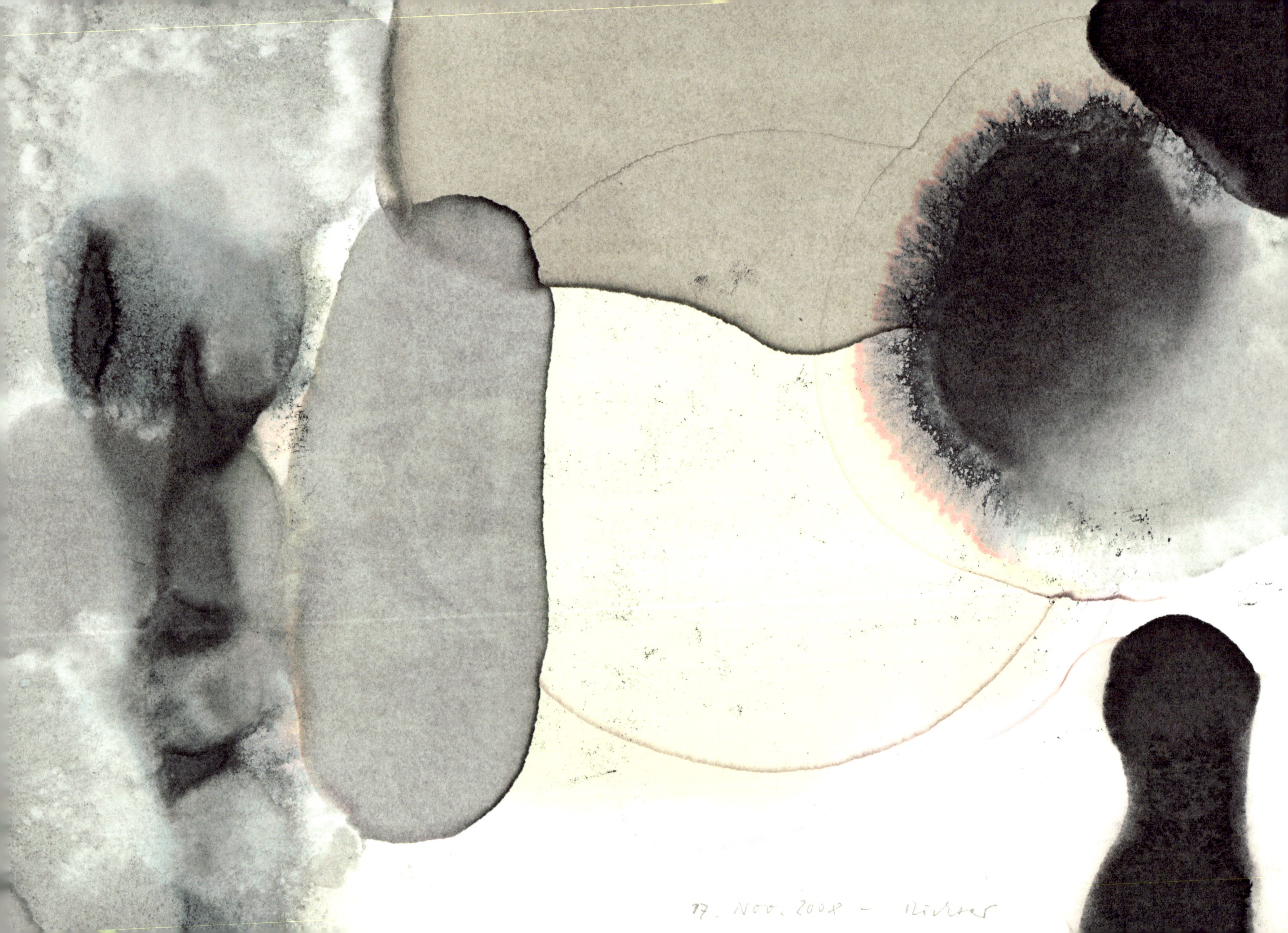
17. Nov. 2008 – Richter

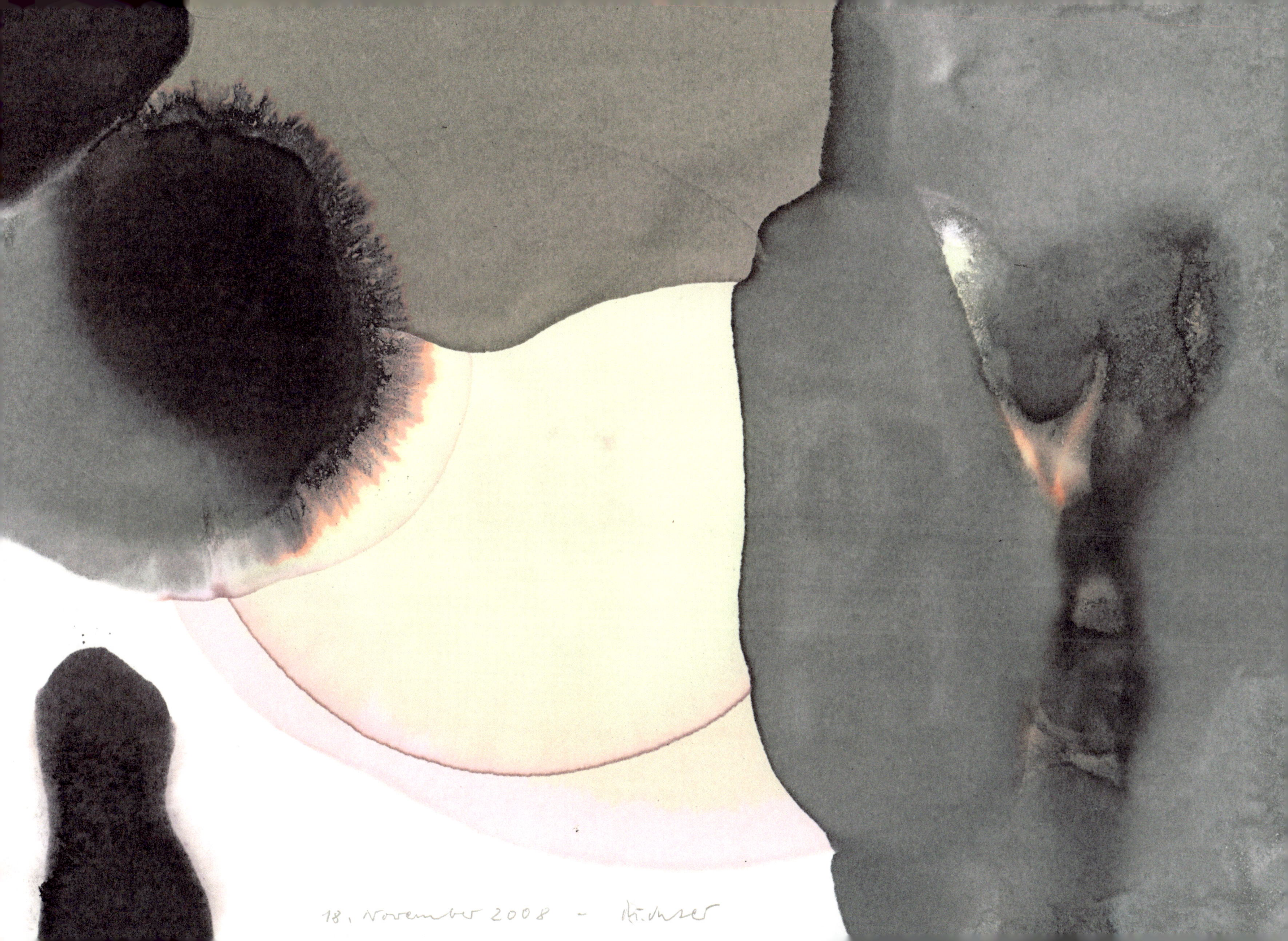
18. November 2008

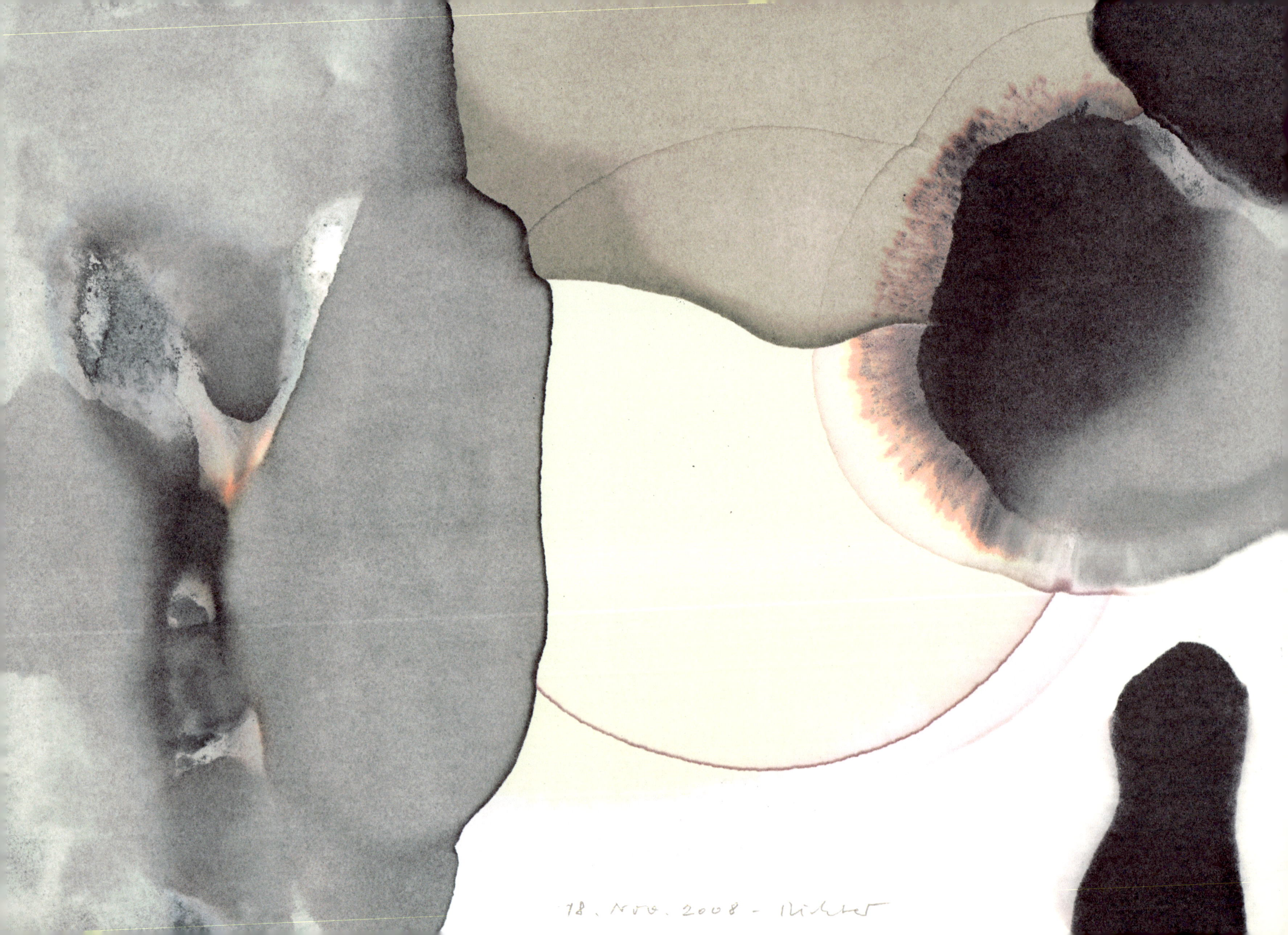
18. Nov. 2008 - Richter

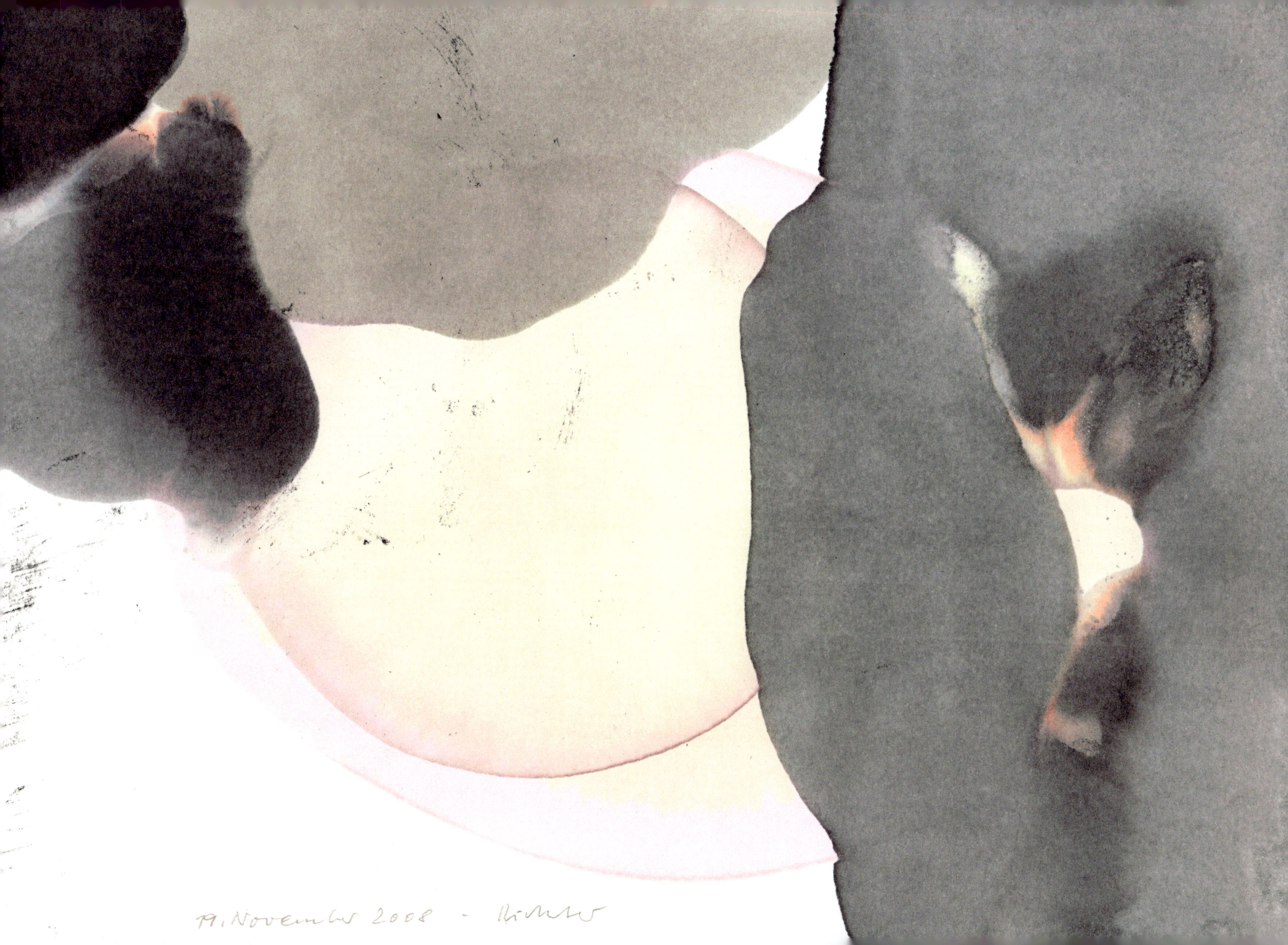
19. November 2008 - Richter

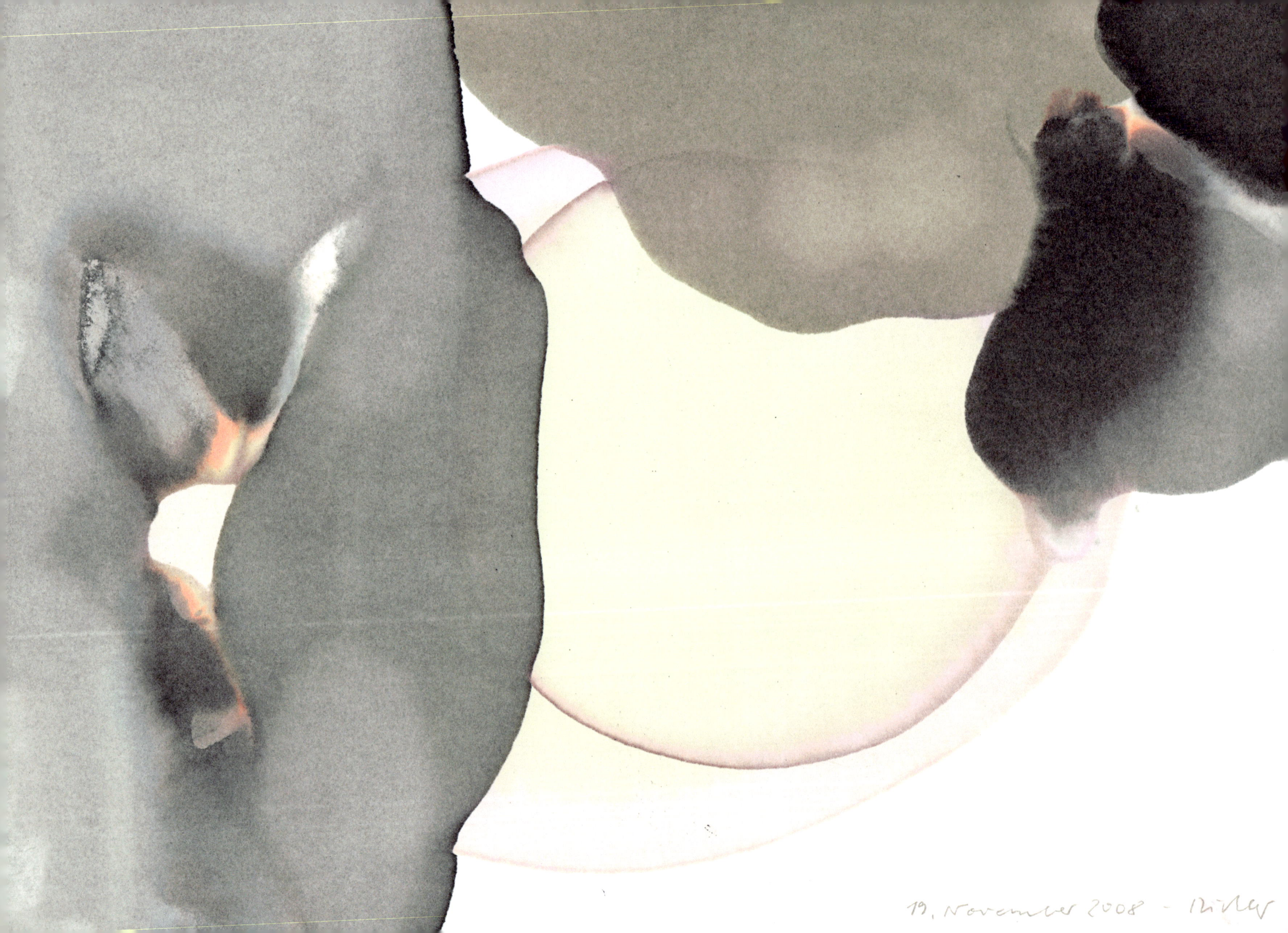
19. November 2008 - Richter

20. NOV. 2008 · Richter.

20. Nov. 2008 - Richter

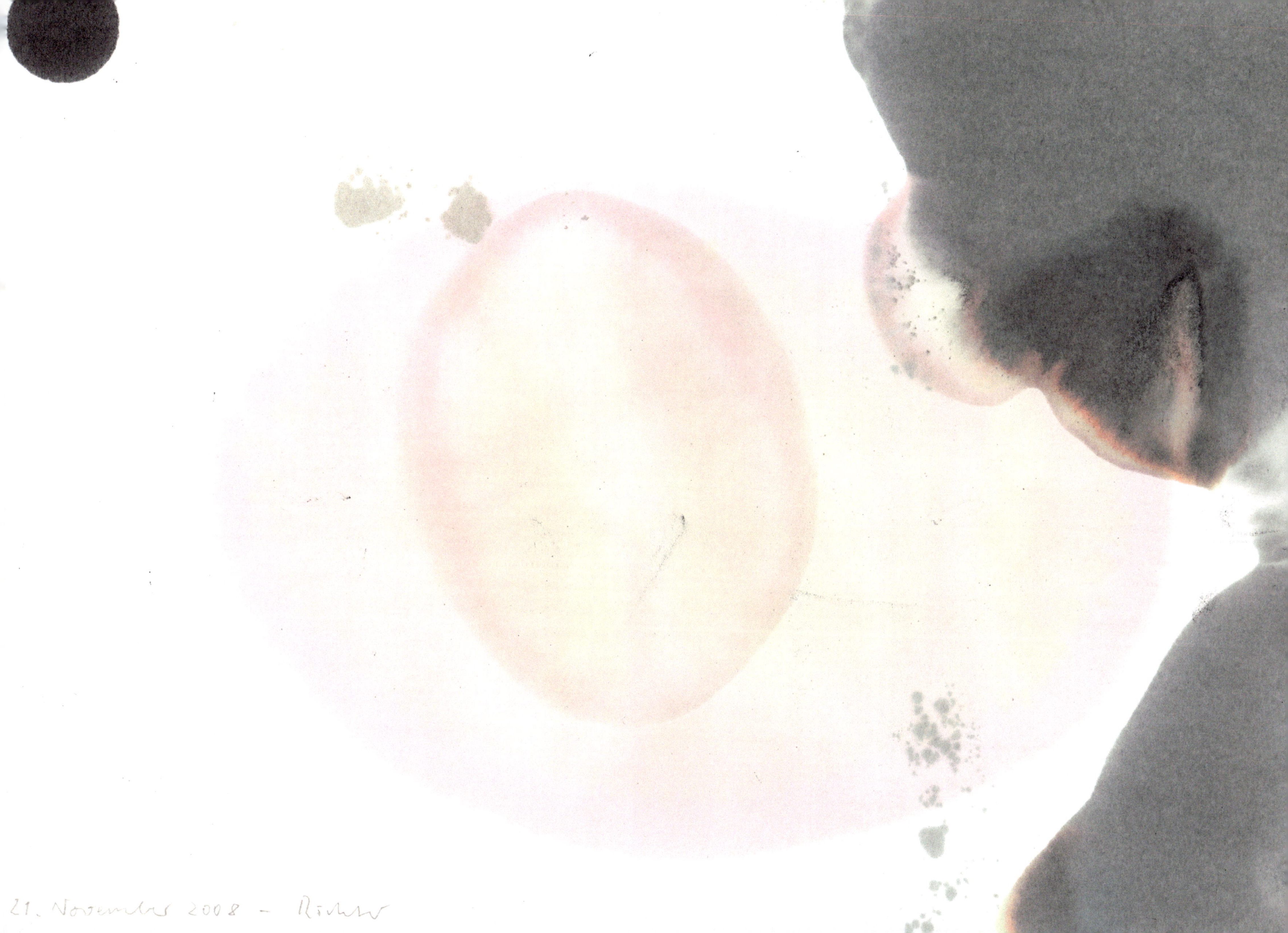
21. November 2008 – Richter

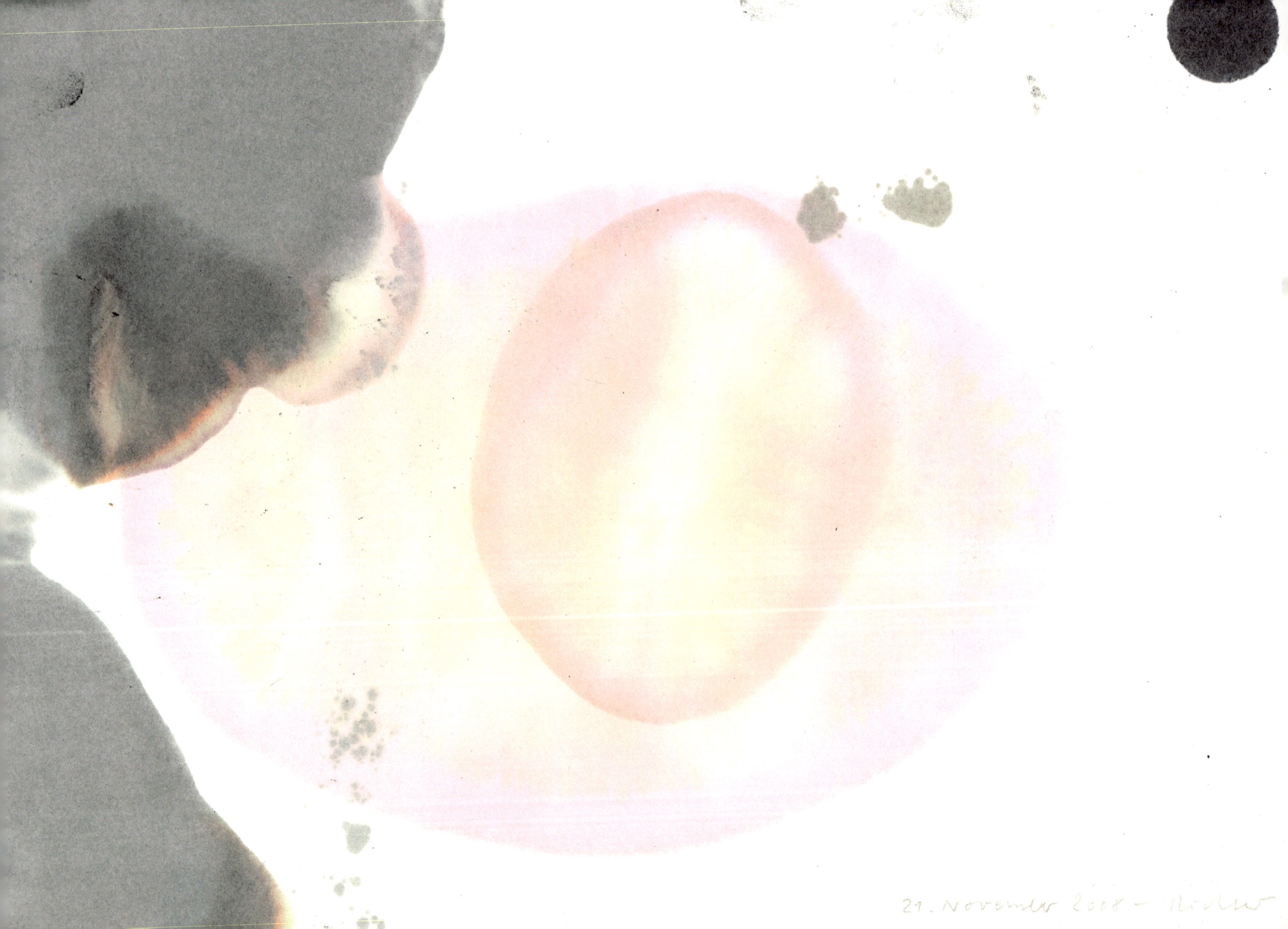
21. November 2008 –

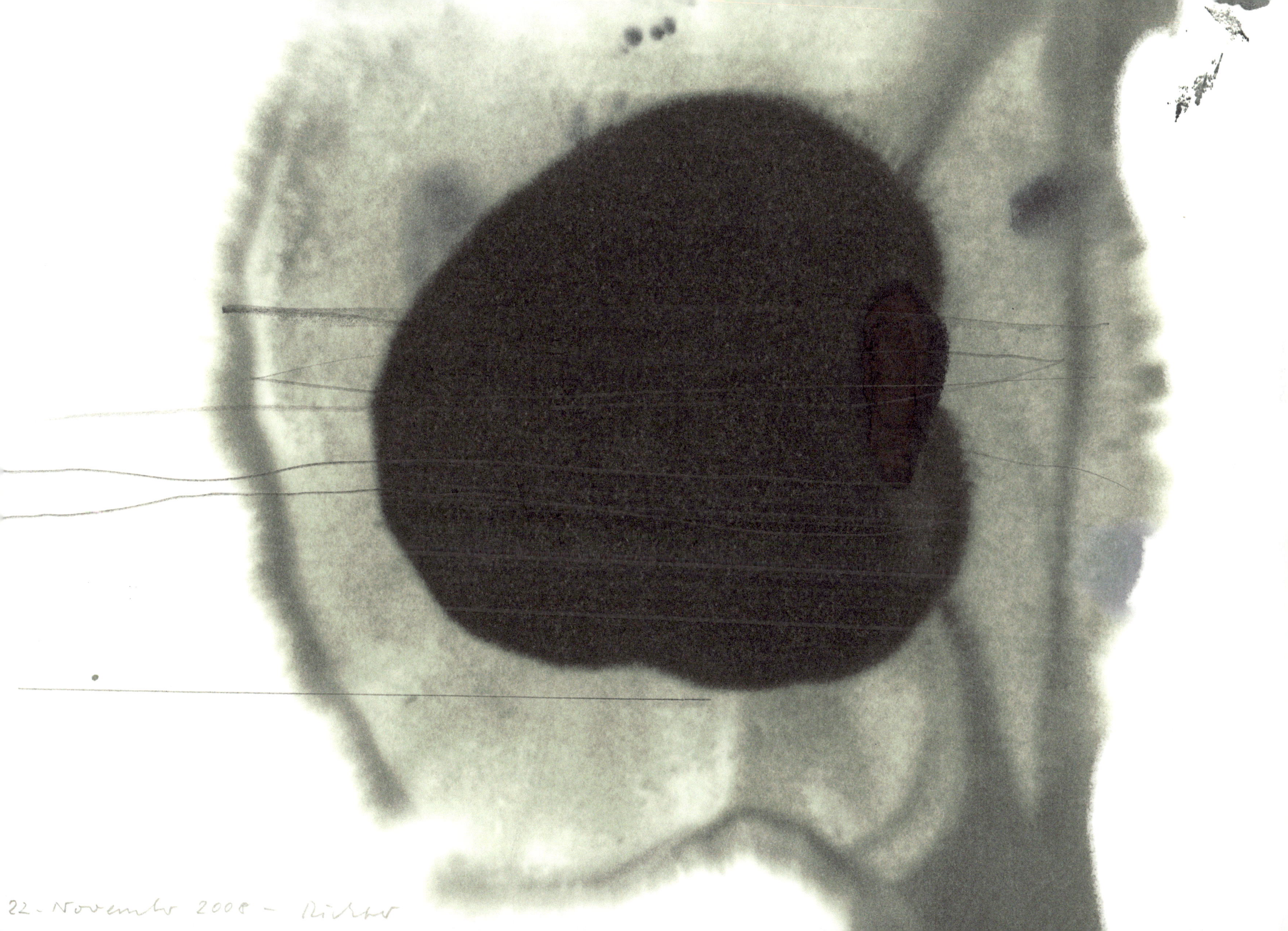
22. November 2008 – Richter

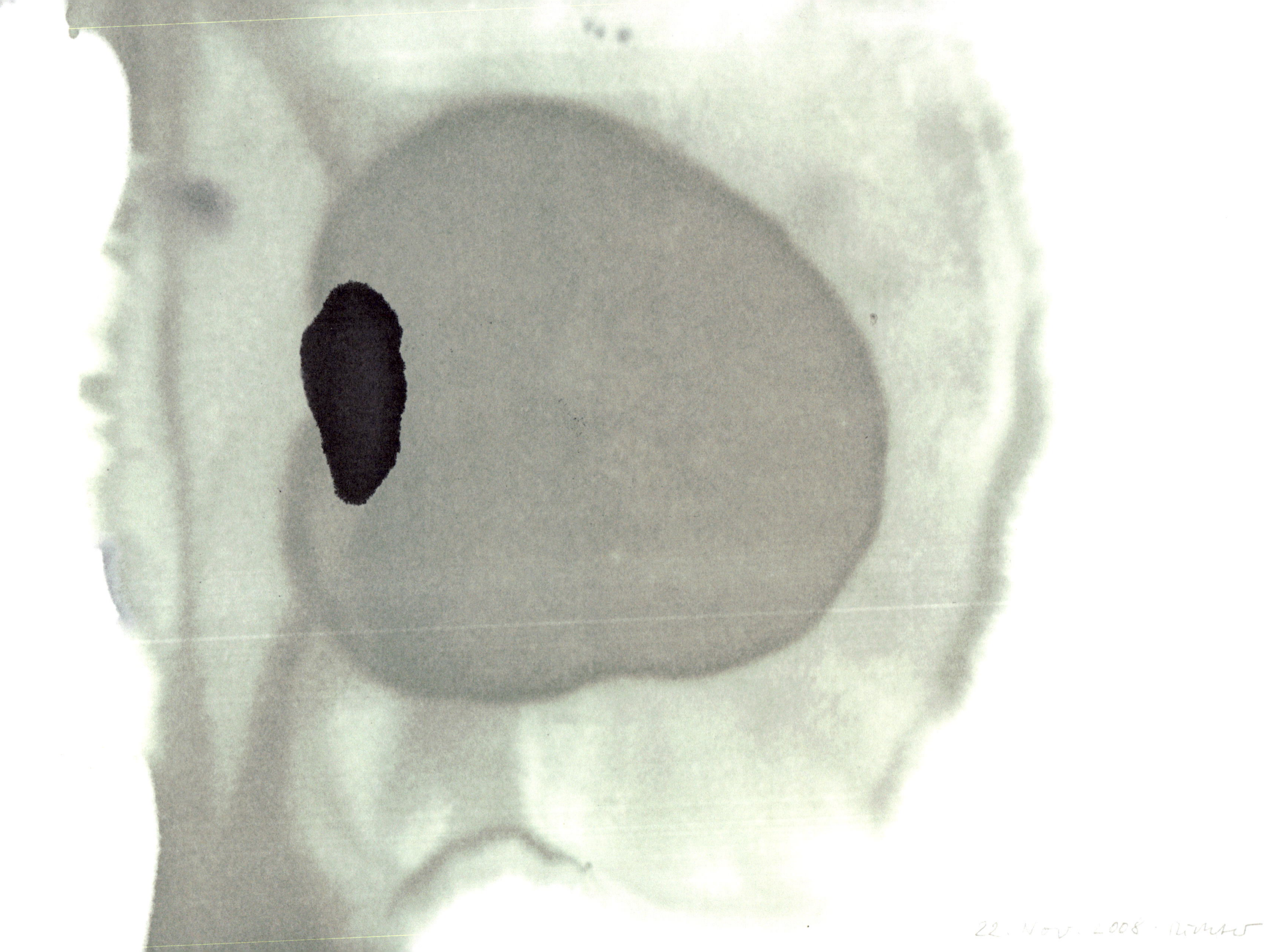
22. Nov. 2008

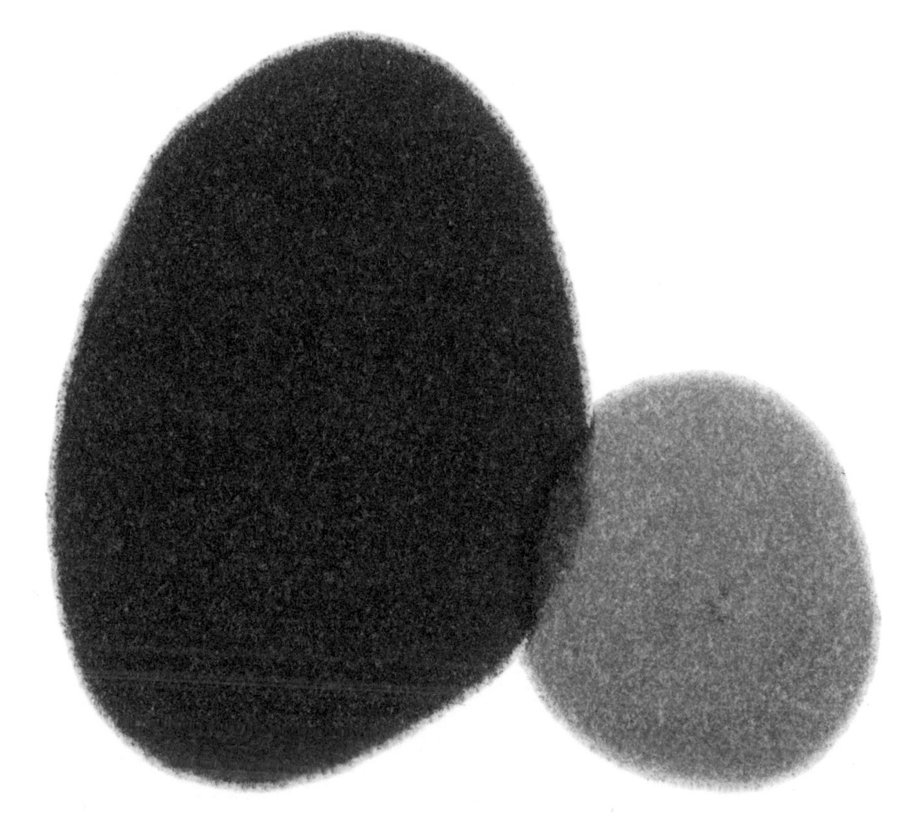

23. Nov. 2008 R.

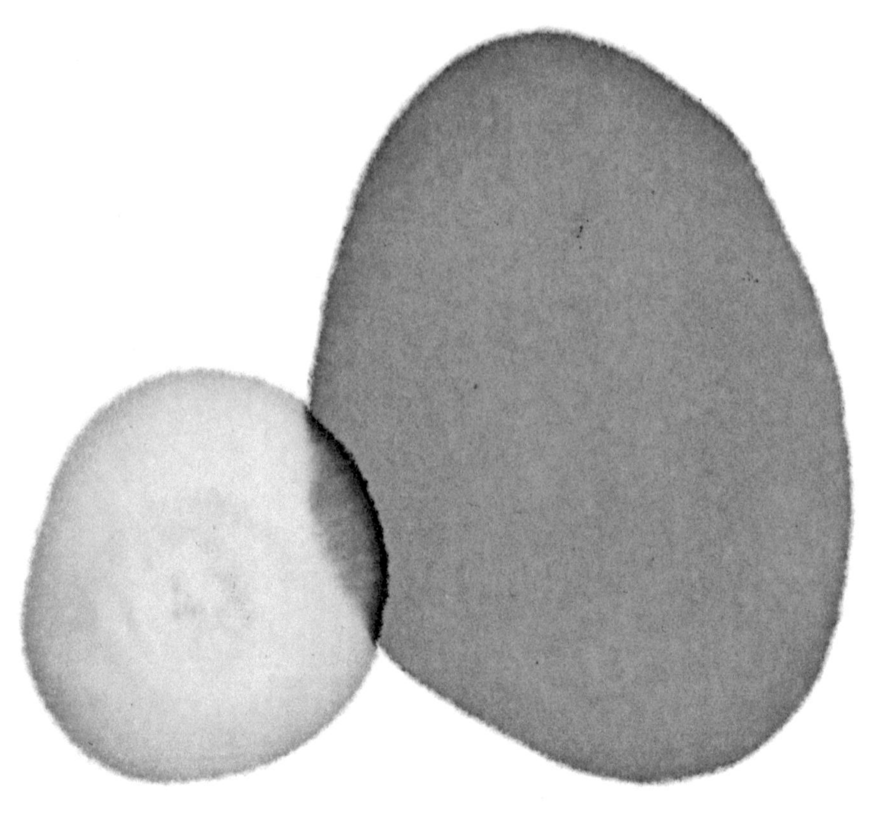

Richter, 23. Nov. 2008

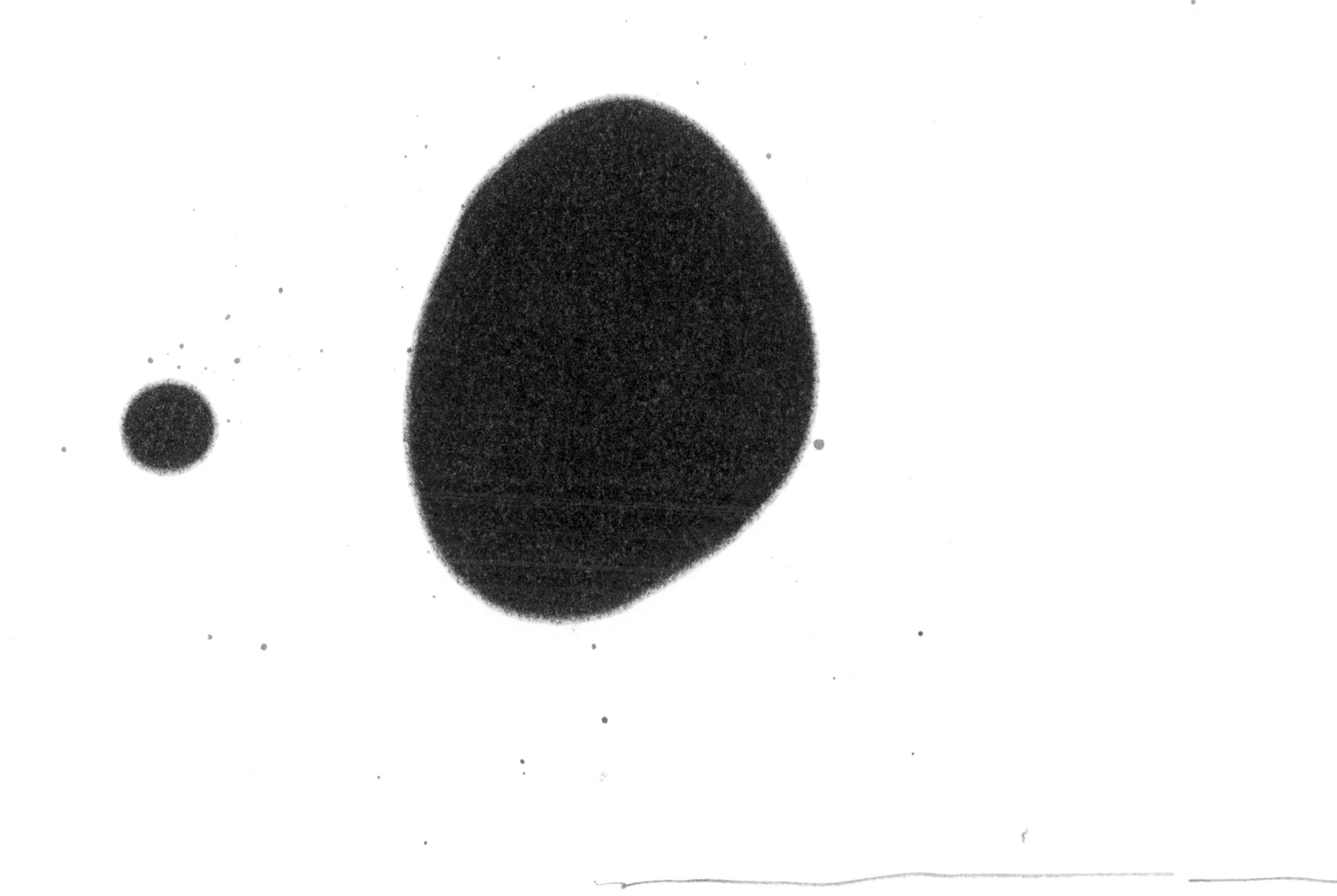

24. Nov. 2008 Richter

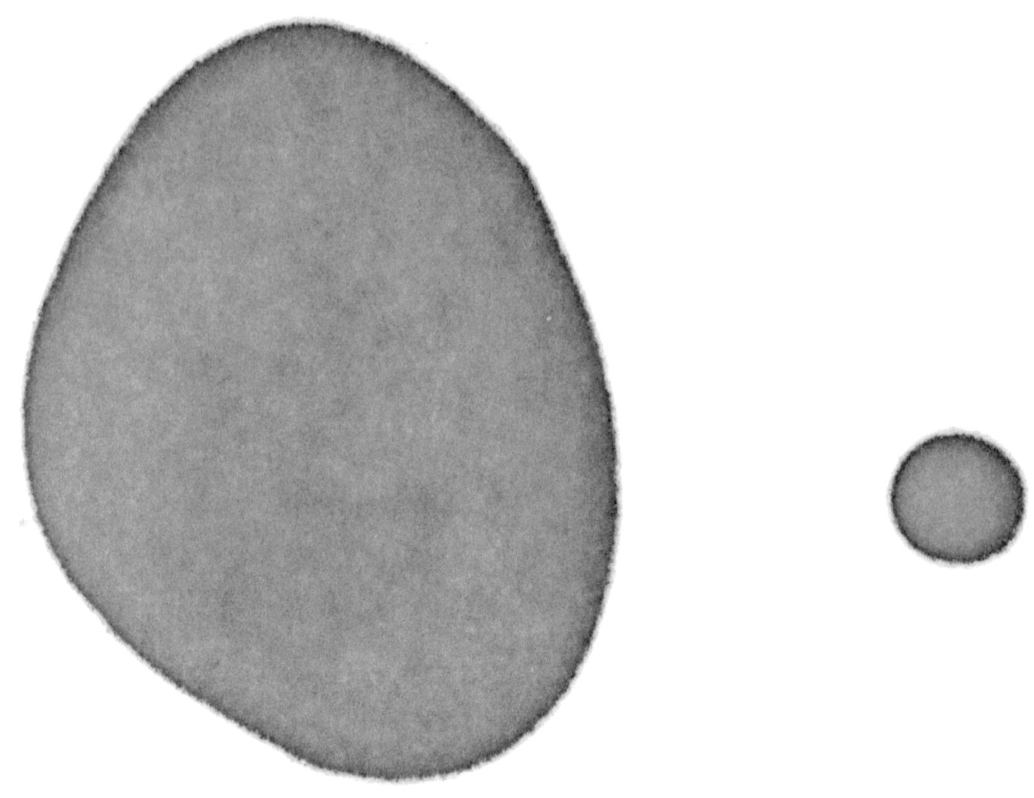

Richter - 24.11.2008

Richter - 25. Nov. 2008

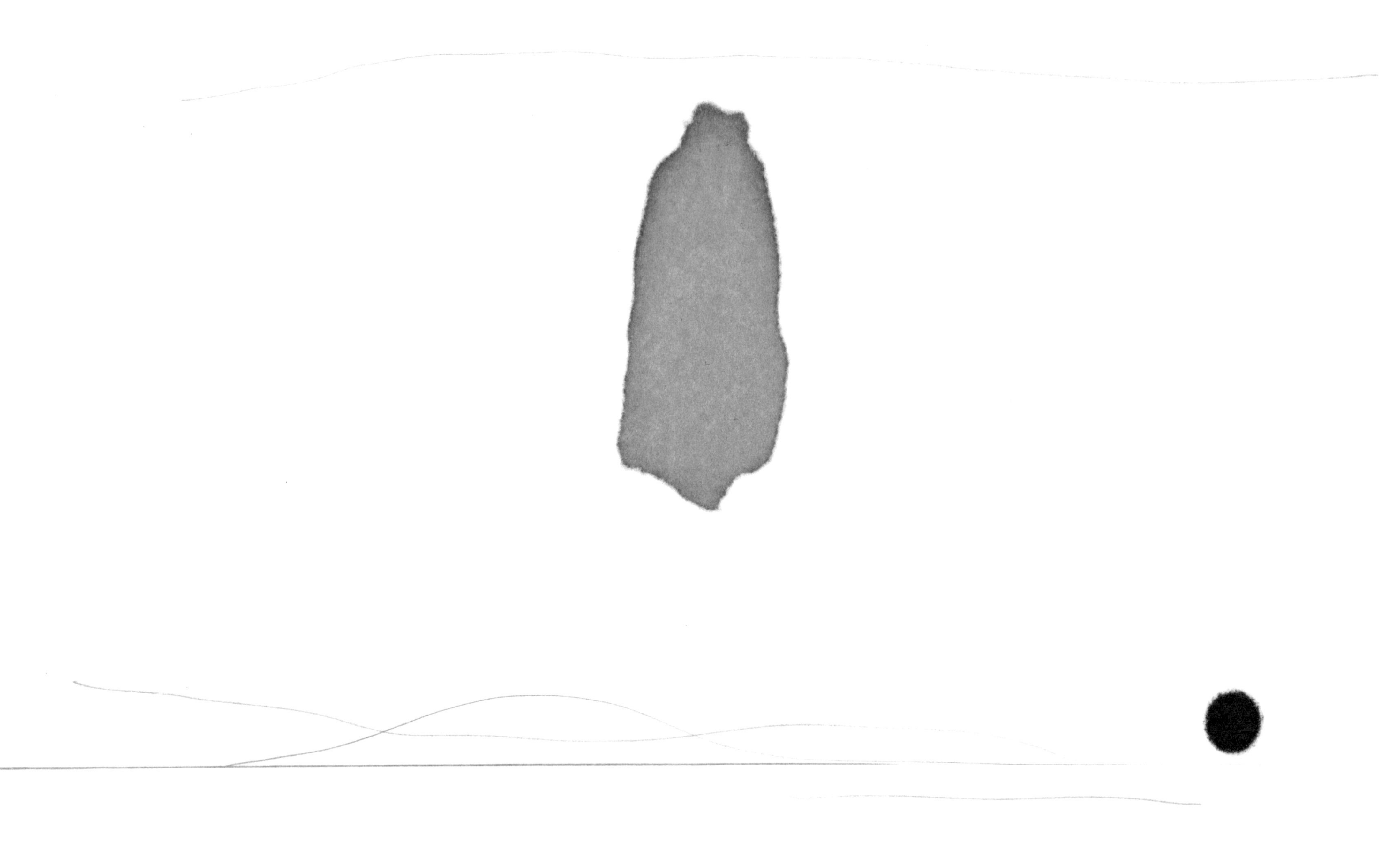

Richter. 24. Nov. 2008

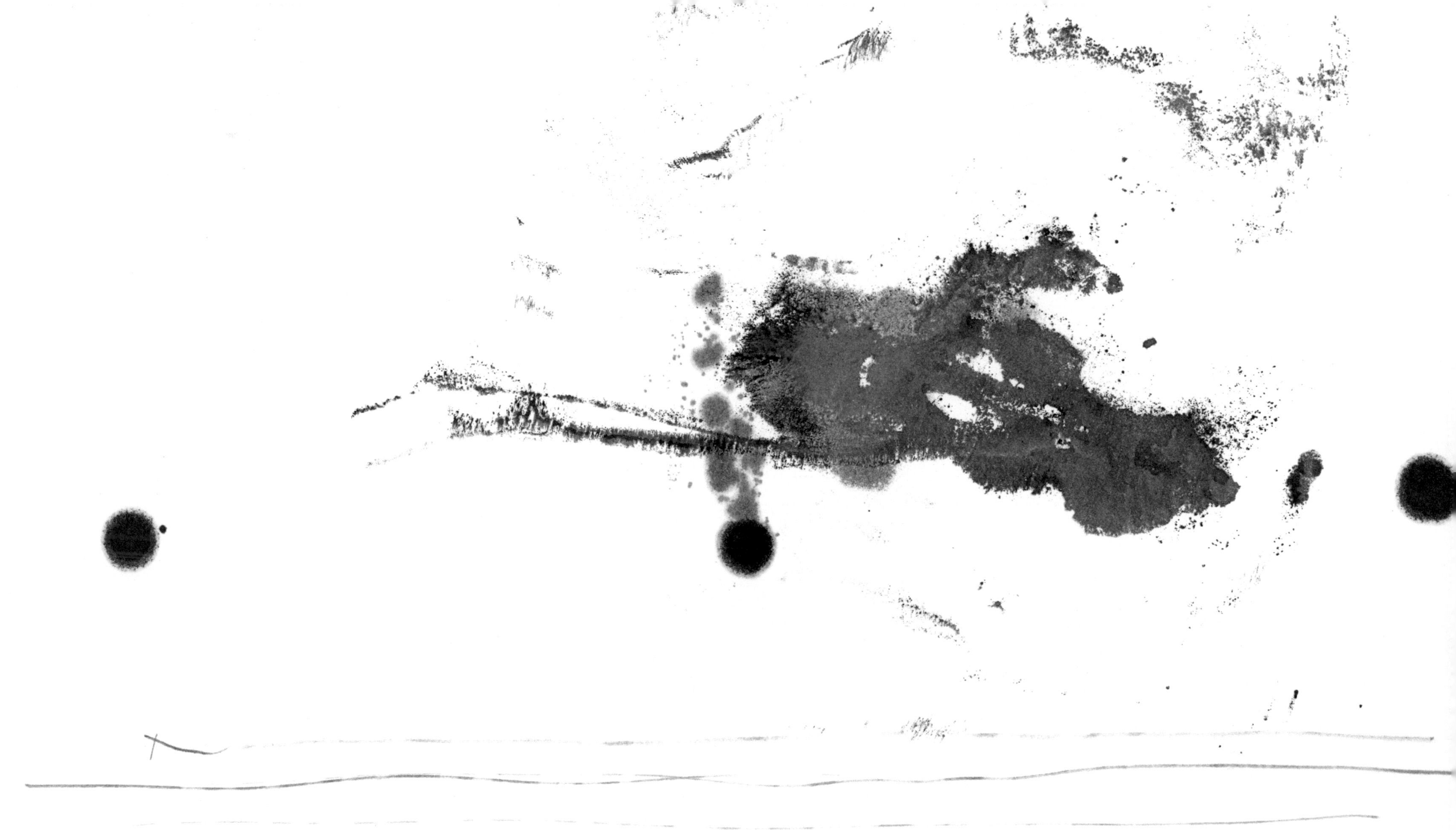

Richter, 26. Nov. 2008

Richter, 26. Nov. 2008

[illegible], 27. Nov. 2008

Richter, 27. November 2008

Richter – 28. Nov. 2008

Richter - 28. November 2008

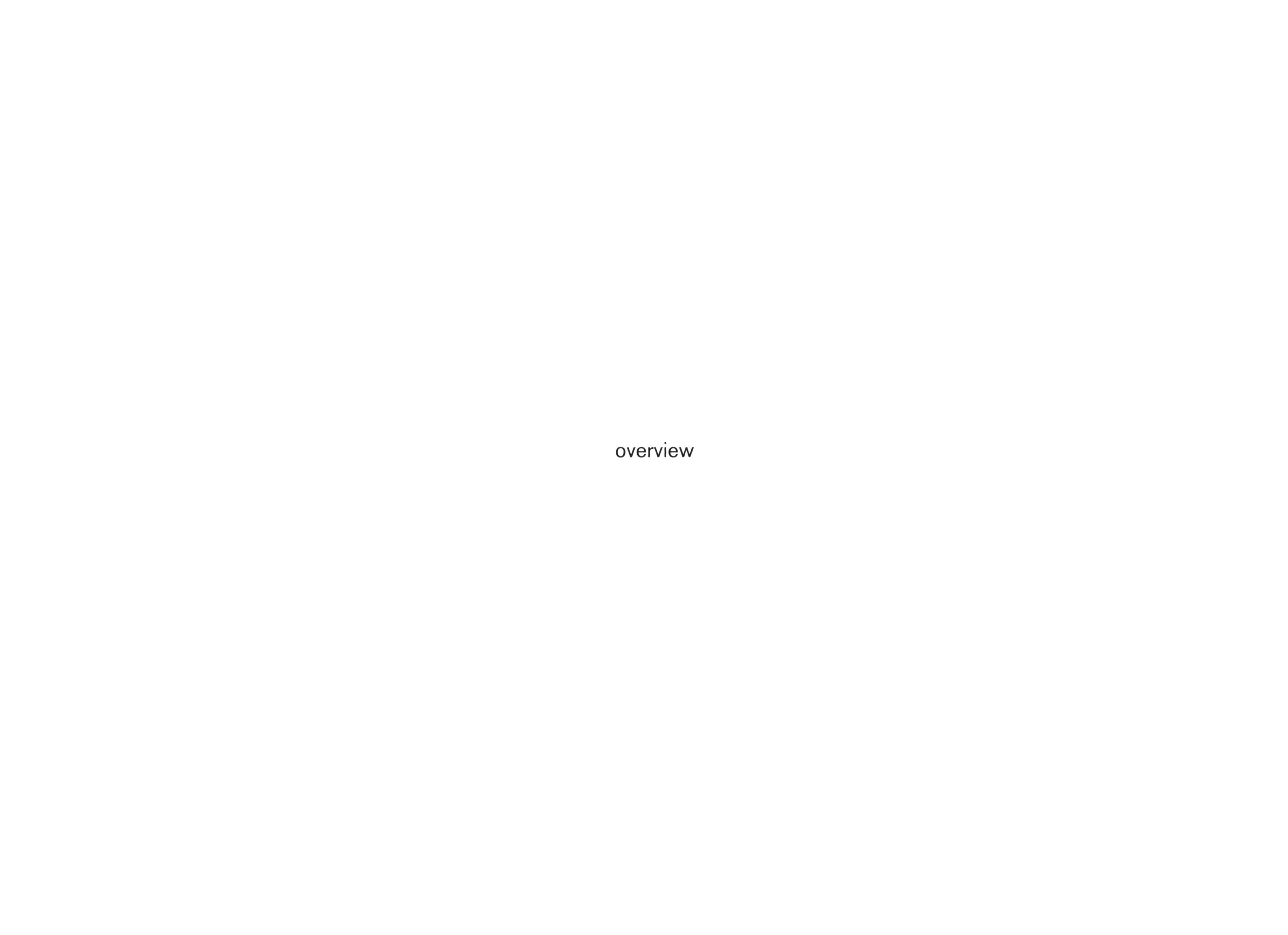
overview

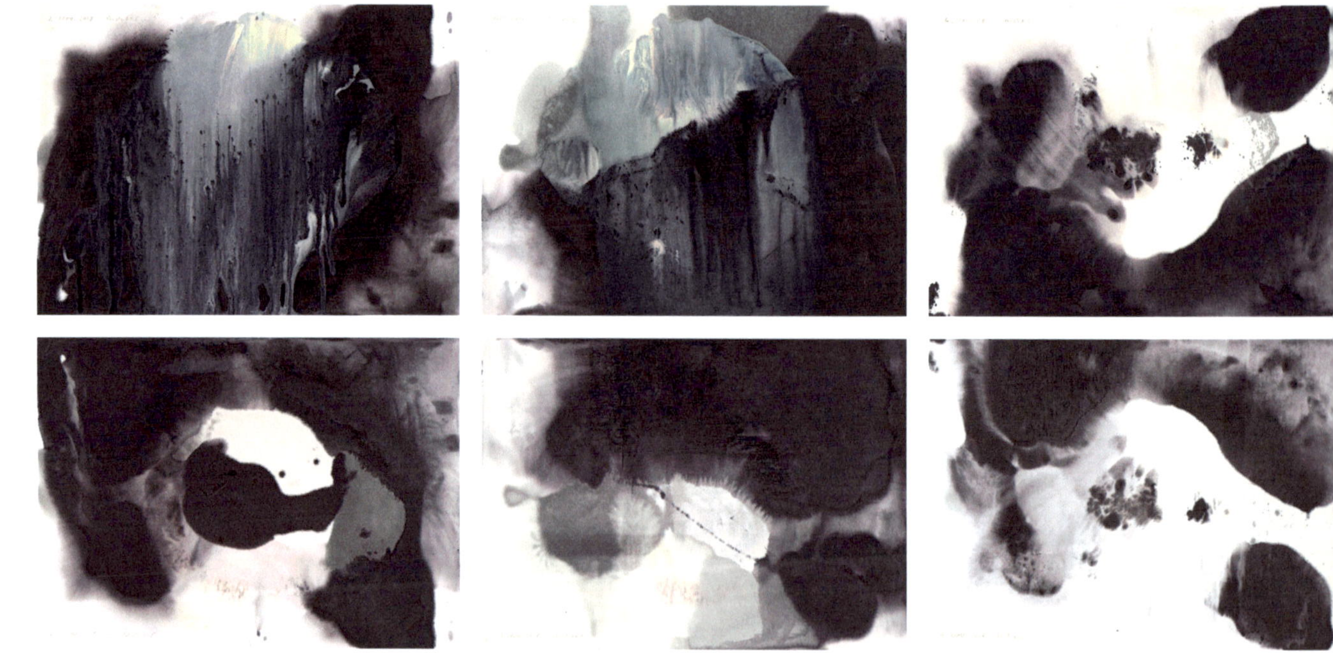

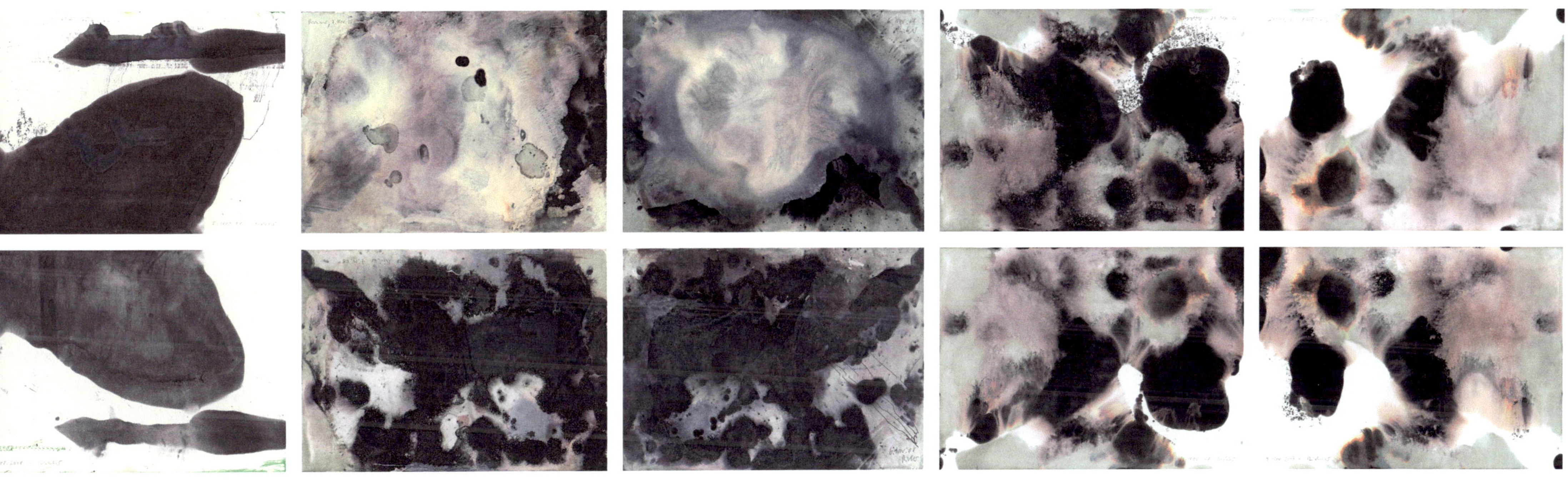

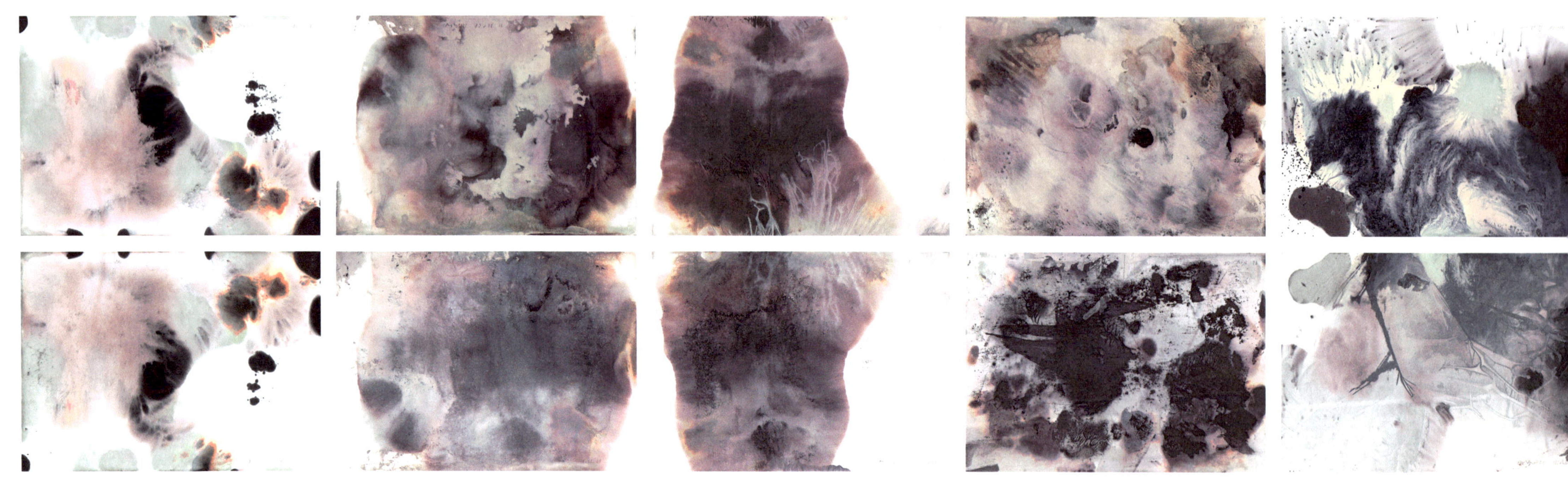

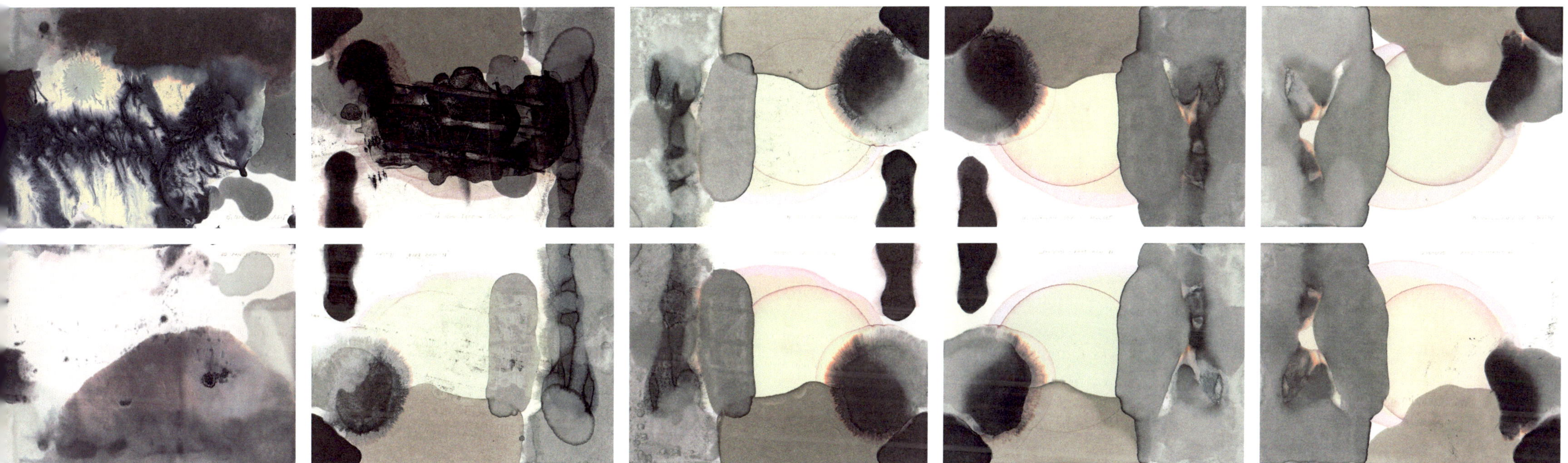

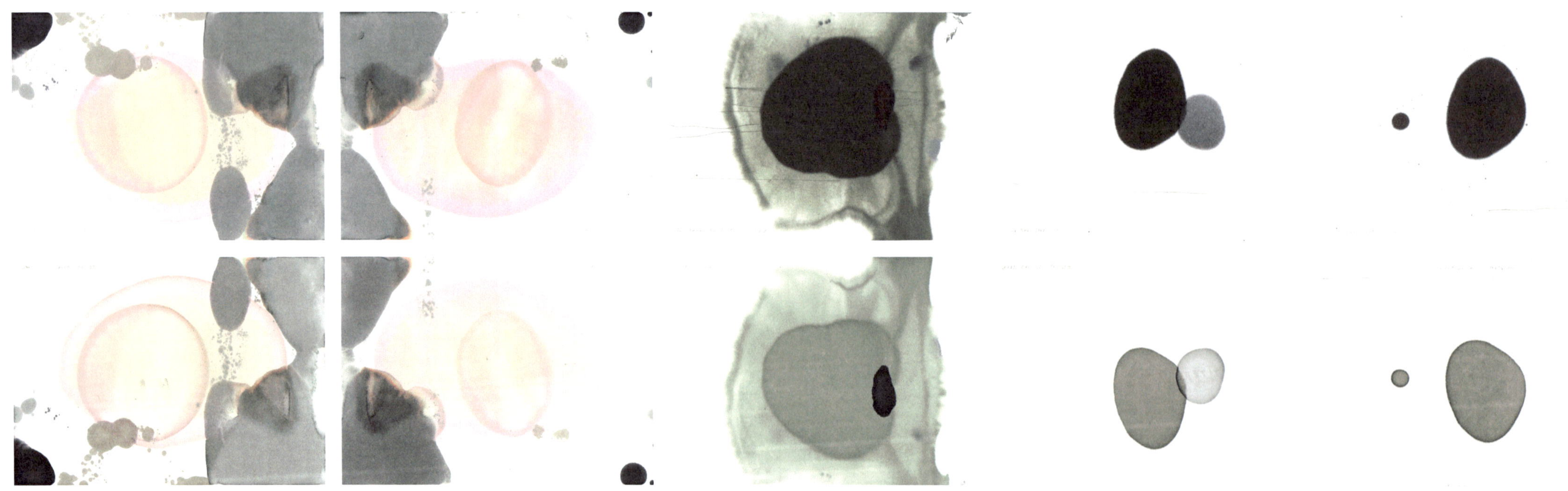

Dieter Schwarz

Gerhard Richter: November

It came as something of a surprise, some years ago, when an early work on paper by Gerhard Richter came to light – his series *Elbe*, made in 1957. Even more surprisingly Richter did not dismiss it – like all the other paintings, watercolours and drawings from his student days in Dresden – but recognised it as part of his œuvre and included it in various exhibitions. *Elbe* consists of thirty-one images, monotypes in black ink on A4 paper. A later series of works in ink, published in this volume and dated November 2008, looks very much like a counterpart by virtue of both its production method and appearance. The blotches, veiled sections, layers and illusionistic openings of *Elbe* are all seen again in the *November* sheets. Whereas there is still a sense of constraint in the handling of the materials in the earlier cycle, *November* is the work of a practised artist, temporarily setting aside experience and knowledge in order to renew the parameters of his own work. For all the external differences, it seems that these two chronologically distant works bespeak the same attitude and approach. One might even suggest that these two cycles demarcate the temporal and conceptual span of Gerhard Richter's drawings and watercolours.

From the 1970s onwards Richter sporadically worked in watercolours but seemed to lose interest in the medium after 1997. The works he produced in 1997 already no longer conformed to tradition, with the watery colours applied to the paper in drips and pools, which he dispersed not only using a brush but also by tipping and moving the sheet around. This interplay of deliberate intervention and the random movement of the liquid paint led to small-format paintings that are quite distinct from the more "drawn" watercolours that Richter was making in the 1970s. Their abstraction had nothing in common with that of his oil paintings, for both the proportions of the compositions and their potential for effects were of a very different order. Nevertheless, Richter remained suspicious of watercolours, for he feared that they might appear too winsome and craftsmanlike, and it may be that this was what henceforth prevented him from succumbing again to the appeal of watercolours.

Ten years later Richter was producing new, innovative works – from a stained-glass window for Cologne Cathedral to vertically stacked panes of glass, which led to further experiments in 2008. He now applied enamel paints to a table-sized sheet of Plexiglas and directed their flow with brushes and spatulas. Before the colours could merge into an indeterminate mass, Richter arrested the process by laying a sheet of glass on the paint and fixing a particular section at a particular moment in time. This led to several groups of paintings behind glass. Thus Richter honed his eye for unforeseen effects and was now prepared to select and accept working methods that he had previously avoided. This in turn saw the making of the *November* series, unplanned, on the margins of a more conventional work process. As he was decanting black Edding marker-pen ink, Richter found himself watching the ink dripping onto some paper. So, toying with this idea, he tipped some ink onto other sheets and started to use a variety of means to manipulate its flow. He thinned it with benzene or acetone and added black tusche and other ingredients; as he did so the colour of the fluid changed, developing reddish and blueish hues. Since the paper Richter used for this was highly absorbent, the ink soaked through to the back of the sheets creating two related, reversed images, one on either side. The inks mixed with solvents then soaked down through the stack of sheets leaving ever fainter marks, which linked the figurations together like echoes. In a few cases Richter applied lacquer to one side of the sheet, or drew pencil lines across the patches of colour, marking particular moments in the flow of shapes. This contemplative game with inks, with Richter leafing forwards and backwards through the sheets, produced twenty-seven two-sided works that follow in a sequence determined by their making. As so often in his long career as a painter, Richter was initially wary of the outcome of this process, set the ensemble aside and postponed his final judgement on it.

One of the distinguishing features of Richter's working methods is that he is rarely, if ever, satisfied with his own initial gesture, and as a rule subjects it to a lengthy process of critical scrutiny, revision and reworking, from which a work ultimately arises whose substance may by now have progressed far beyond what might have originally appeared to be the artist's intention. This is particularly apparent in the case of certain paintings that Richter photographed at various stages during their making. In so doing, he is no different to other painters from the past who have favoured a similar form of self-critique. However, in Richter's case there is another aspect to this process, which can be seen very well in the *November* sheets and which could be described as a synthetic reworking. At the same time, it would be wrong to view this as a concept or a method, for the nature of this post-production process is always different, depending on the circumstances of the work in question. Reference has already been made here to the discovery of the *Elbe* cycle. In order to exhibit it in its entirety, facsimiles had to be made of the backs of the seven sheets that had been worked on both sides. Richter subsequently observed that few viewers were able to distinguish the original sheets from the ink-jet reproductions – in an instance of the unintentional confusion of reality and its likeness. When he then returned to *November* three years after its making, he had a complete set of facsimiles made because this was the only way to view both sides of the twenty-seven sheets at the same time and to come to any conclusions regarding the entire series.

The ensuing sequence, with its regular alternation of recto and verso, conveyed the sense of an almost mechanical process in the virtually symmetrical pairs of images. This series of mirror-image situations gave rise to an interesting factor that Richter had not hitherto been able to deploy so directly in either his drawings or watercolours. In these "reflections" each motif was juxtaposed with its own mirror image, in other words, a particular mimetic relationship ensued, in the sense that the likenesses do not replicate a motif in the usual way but re-present it in reverse. At the same time, the likeness is so faithful that it is hard to distinguish it from the original motif, indeed the relationship can be reversed – the original and the likeness can be interchanged or become impossible to tell apart. Richter has used reflections in various ways in his work. The pose of the painter checking the accuracy of his own work in a hand-held mirror is familiar from photographs. And in addition to the crystal clear or coloured mirrors that are interspersed in amongst the paintings in Richter's catalogue raisonné, there are also apparent reflections included in the photographs that make up *128 Details from a Picture* (1978) and in the picture sequences in his photo-book *Eis* (2011). The book *War Cut* (2004) is constructed from enlarged details of a painting, which are arranged in a complex, self-mirroring sequence.

In his *November* suite Richter now had material to hand that was by definition an invitation to incorporate the notion of reflection into the work. Not only were there sheets with a mirror image of the motif on the reverse; in some cases the ink that had soaked through layers of sheets created what looked like visual echoes. These factors led to a multiplicity of internal connections that provided a structure for the sequence of images. Nevertheless, Richter's manipulation of the given sequence was distinctly restrained: for instance, November 2nd (recto) is placed upside down, disturbing the regularity of the mirror-image connections. In addition to this, the obscuring over-painting of this same sheet and of November 3rd draws attention to the differences between the two, rather than to any repetition. In the case of the pairs of sheets dated November 4th and 5th, the verso images are again rotated by 180°; it also appears that the sequence of front and back has been reversed in the case of the latter. The given reflections are thus just the point of departure for an interlocking web of connections, which in turn creates simultaneity from a temporal and material sequence. In the same way that original and facsimile are barely distinguishable, any distinctive qualities in the different ink markings are all but impossible to discern – with the initial disposition on one side and copy, duplicate and replica on the other. The facsimiles allowed Richter to progress beyond the material form of the ink drawings. Although these form the foundations of the sequence, the process of reproduction sees them shifting to a different level. Richter engages not only with this fact but also with the meaning it acquires in a syntactical context; his interest is in the visible phenomenon, not in its material constitution as a secondary likeness, nor in its primary essence. He is not dependent on a unique handwriting, that is to say, on the original, for reproduction provides him with a means to make connections between a chance detail and other details and to instigate correlations. The notion of synthesis mentioned earlier here thus refers not to drawing strands together in the sense of making them legible but rather the aesthetic resolution of raw reality and facticity in a work of art.

That visibility comes before the essence, that it does not even have a symbolic relationship to it is also true of photography, which in itself makes the link between the *November* sheets and Richter's working methods as a painter. In the early 1960s he discovered that photography could serve him as a tool to break free of the compositional methods he had been taught, as a way of avoiding or at least minimising creative decisions and of increasing the level of indeterminacy in his paintings. The camera as a mechanical, picture-making instrument that does not see, that merely captures images, supplied compositions that were not already interpreted, calculated and constructed according to certain hierarchies. Initially these photographs were no more than a specifically configured mass of grey tones on a plane, which could be read – on an abstract level – as figures and shapes. Having once before thrown in his lot with the likeness for his own work, Richter did the same thing again in these much later works in ink, however different they may appear. When Richter, pursuing his interest in paintings behind glass, in fact chose to explore a side path, away from the beaten track of large-format abstractions, he did so in the hope of arriving by a different route at pictures that could give visible form to something hitherto unknown. There is no limit to possible colour combinations and the principle behind them is thus not so far removed from that of photography, which also has to deal with the limitlessness of the depictable. The transferring of enamel paints to panes of glass is just as clearly not painting as the game with inks on paper and is not presented as such by Richter. These processes have more in common with photography, where a section of reality in the shape of a ray of light hits a plate and is captured there.

As we have seen, chance is merely a stepping stone for Richter, for his work is about moving some distance beyond the material fact, which is initially temporal, before it becomes a matter of reproduction, relocation, reorganisation and ultimately an aesthetic entity. This distance can be understood in terms of the fictionalisation that accompanies the work process. An unremarkable detail, namely the retrospective dating of the *November* sheets, may be used to explain this. While the work does indeed date back to 2008, the sheets were not – as the dates suggest – made in the period 2 to 28 November. According to convention, the dates given by an artist to a cycle of works cast it in the role of an artistic journal. By contract, Richter's dating of this series was a retrospective decision, which presents the sequence of images as a narrative. This fictive sequence is entirely at odds with the actual making of the cycle, which will not have taken nearly as long as a month – in view of the volatility of the solvents, groups of sheets must have been made in quick succession. Richter thus used the dates he gave the sheets symbolically to suggest the duration of the work's making. The idea that the cycle came about during the course of a whole month in autumn serves as an atmospheric metaphor and encourages the viewer to respond to the sheets, like music, in terms of that particular time-span. *November* ends with bleak patches of colour that stand on the paper like isolated sounds in a piece by John Cage – abandoned, disconnected but momentarily regarded by the viewer in conjunction with each other in the context created by the artist. Given that the *November* sheets talk of their making, Cage's words, in the following example, revolve around their making too, around the question of potential order and meaning, which perhaps can only be found in the mirror image. This passage from Cage's late prose work *Anarchy*, conveys a sense of Richter's work better than any description ever could:

noT
The
nOt
thE
Processes
mereLy
Order
In order
anyThing

First published in 2013 by Heni Publishing, London
in a limited edition of 800 copies

Second edition published in 2015
by Heni Publishing, London

Concept and layout: Gerhard Richter
Translation from the German: Fiona Elliott
Typography: Silke Fahnert and Uwe Koch, Cologne
Lithography and production:
Printmanagement Plitt, Oberhausen

Printed in Germany

A catalogue record for this book is available from
the British Library.

ISBN 978-0-9930103-1-6